Diocese of Owensboro

A Celebration of the Catholic Church in Western Kentucky

Published by

MESSENGER-INQUIRER

a division of Paxton Media Group
Robert Morris, Publisher

ISBN   978-0-9789166-8-8

On the Cover: Easter Vigil 2010

Parishioners stand during the Easter Vigil at St. Stephen Cathedral in Owensboro on Saturday, April 3, 2010. Easter Vigil is the first official celebration of the Resurrection of Jesus. During this service catechumens are baptized and adult candidates are received into full Communion with the Church. It is held in the hours of darkness between sunset on Holy Saturday and sunrise on Easter Day. *Messenger-Inquirer photo by Gary Emord-Netzley*

ACKNOWLEDGEMENTS

Project Staff

Beck Schofield Glenn, Editor

John Shelton, Graphic Design

Marty Jackson, Carrie Jewell, Jessica Ling, Heather Goatee and Amy Ellis, Production Assistance

Karen Dunlop, Dianne Frey and Amber Hendrix, Book Sales

Special Thanks

This book is a collection of photos and memories from the life of the Catholic Church in western Kentucky.

The Most Rev. William Francis Medley, fourth Bishop of the Diocese of Owensboro, deserves gratitude for his support of this project.

The vast majority of the photographs in this volume come from the collection in the archives of the Diocese of Owensboro, housed at the Catholic Pastoral Center in Owensboro, Ky. Diocesan Archivist Sister Emma Cecilia Busam, O.S.U., and archival volunteer Brett Mills were welcoming guides to the vast amount of information meticulously recorded and saved in their care. Mel Howard, Director of the Diocesan Office of Communications and Editor of The Western Kentucky Catholic newspaper, was a patient tutor in the fundamentals of Catholic traditions and instrumental to the project. Thanks also to Diocesan Chancellor Sister Joseph Angela Boone, O.S.U., Assistant to the Chancellor Ernie Taliaferro, Administrative Assistant in the Communications Office Tami Schneider and Director of the Diocesan Office of Faith Formation Elaine Robertson for all of their time spent proofreading the finished product.

A special thanks also to the individuals from around western Kentucky who contributed photographs to make sure their home parish was adequately represented in the book. Through this project, digital copies of the photos you contributed will become a permanent part of the Diocesan archives for future generations of Catholics to enjoy.

All contributors are acknowledged by name with the material they submitted.

INTRODUCTION

For a non-Catholic, the task of compiling a pictorial history of the Diocese of Owensboro seemed a daunting one. To say I was nervous about starting the project would be a colossal understatement. I fretted about offending someone in my ignorance right up until my first face-to-face meeting with a diocesan staff member. I laid my fears on the table. He responded with acceptance and reassurance that mistakes made in ignorance would simply be corrected. He began my introduction to the Catholic faith by explaining the seven sacraments of the church and how they are the foundation of all the beliefs and traditions for the Catholic Church. He even answered my questions on a random variety of topics that I had read about before the meeting. Our discussions that first day about the basics of Catholicism became the basis for the organization of this book.

During that first meeting, I was graciously invited to attend the upcoming Mass of Chrism to be held at the Owensboro Sportscenter. I attended with some Catholic friends and witnessed the blessing of the Chrism to be used in all the parishes of the diocese for Baptisms, ordinations and other ceremonies throughout the next year. I also had the privilege of hearing Bishop William Francis Medley address the assembled crowd. Bishop Medley has an aura of charisma – and such an engaging smile – that I think would have caused him to stand out from the crowd even if he had not been wearing the unique vestments of his office. He impressed me as a man of great faith and open love of God and the people who are the Catholic Church in western Kentucky.

"The whole liturgical life of the Church revolves around the Eucharistic sacrifice and the sacraments. There are seven sacraments in the Church: Baptism, Confirmation or Chrismation, Eucharist, Penance, Anointing of the Sick, Holy Orders, and Matrimony (From The Catechism of the Catholic Church, no. 1113)." As the liturgical life of the Church revolves around the sacraments, so does the daily life of Catholics. Because of the central role of the sacraments in Catholic beliefs and practices, the images in this book are organized to focus on each sacrament in turn. Additional sections include images commemorating the men and women called to live a consecrated life, photographs that illustrate the importance of a quality Catholic education and a final section documenting the many more ways the Catholic faith touches the daily lives of Catholics and non-Catholics alike.

– Beck Schofield Glenn, Editor

THE FORTY MARTYRS

When a group of 40 priests – mostly from Louisville – learned in 1937 that they were to stay in western Kentucky to build the new Diocese of Owensboro, they named themselves "The Forty Martyrs." In 2010, at the age of 100, Father Charles Denardi was the only living member of that original group and still resided in the diocese. In this photo, the Knights of Columbus of Grayson County honored Father Charles DeNardi with a surprise, belated 100th year birthday party at Carmel Home in Owensboro on March 27, 2010. A Fourth Degree Honorary Membership was bestowed upon Father DeNardi. DeNardi started the Knights of Columbus in Leitchfield in the 1970s and was their first Chaplain. On behalf of the Knights, Dale Darst of St. Paul Parish presented a wooden plaque to Father DeNardi, on which was engraved, "Rev. Charles A. DeNardi, Born December 25, 1909. On this 27th Day of March 2010, we come together with you to celebrate your belated 100th Birthday. We simply want to take the time to thank you for your many years of service to the Diocese of Owensboro. You were one of the great pioneers that allowed the Diocese of Owensboro to be born. We also thank you for your years of service to the parishes in Grayson County. Through your years of service and your never-ending devotion to God our Father, Jesus, His Son, and the Holy Spirit, you have given comfort and strength to many. We pray that God will continue to bless you, and continue His work through you. May God bless you always! The Knights of Columbus, Fr. Carroll White Council 6743 and Fr. Michael J. McGivney Assembly 3021." Present at the surprise gathering were: Seated, from left, Father Charles Denardi and Dale Darst; second row, from left, Father Marty Hayes, Otto Ballou, James Clemons, and Father Brian Johnson; third row, from left, Danny Harris, Joe Ruther and Raymond Darst. *Information submitted by Sister Andrea Niehaus, D.C.J., and photo submitted by Dale Darst*

Baptism
One of three Sacraments of Christian Initiation

For Catholics, the Sacrament of Baptism is the first of three Sacraments of Christian initiation. Baptism is the first step in a lifelong journey of commitment and discipleship. The Catechism of the Catholic Church states: "Baptism is necessary for salvation for those to whom the Gospel has been proclaimed and who have had the possibility of asking for this sacrament."

In Catholic teachings, baptism plays an essential role in salvation. Baptism is the Church's way of celebrating and enacting the embrace of God who first loved us from the moment of our conception. Baptism celebrates a family's and a community's experience of that love in the baptized.

The Catholic Church traditionally baptizes the infant children of members within a few days or weeks of birth. Baptism is a sign and means of God's love that frees the infant from original sin and communicates divine life. The church holds that there need not be a conscious acceptance of the sacrament by the baptized infant because assurances are required from the parents or godparents that the child will be given the benefit of a Catholic upbringing.

> Jesus answered, "Amen, amen, I say to you, no one can enter the kingdom of God without being born of water and Spirit. What is born of flesh is flesh and what is born of spirit is spirit.
>
> *John 3:5-6*

Through the Rite of Christian Initiation of Adults (RCIA), adults and older children are gradually introduced to the Roman Catholic faith and way of life. These Catechumens, as they are called during an extended period of instruction, learn the principles of the Christian religion with a view to Baptism. An adult seeking to join the church who has already been validly baptized in another Christian faith is called a candidate and is not baptized a second time.

In the name of the Father, and of the Son, and of the Holy Spirit. Amen.
Sign of the Cross

RECEIVED
Bishop Francis R. Cotton at a Mass at Camp Breckenridge near Morganfield in the fall of 1951. Bishop Cotton confirming soldiers into the church as their sponsors lay on hands from behind. *Submitted by Diocesan Archives*

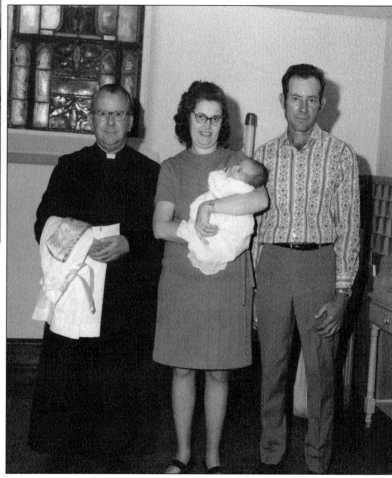

HOLY GUARDIAN ANGELS PARISH
The 1963 First Communion class of Holy Guardian Angels Parish, Irvington, with Father Arnold Meiring, pastor, and an unidentified sister. *Submitted by Holy Guardian Angels Parish*

BLESSED
Father Marvin McAtee with Peggy and Bob McCarthy after the Baptism of their daughter Kathleen on Nov. 2, 1975 at St. Elizabeth Church in Curdsville. *Submitted by Peggy McCarthy*

CHRIST BAPTIZED

This sculpture depicts Jesus' Baptism by John the Baptist. *Submitted by Diocesan Archives*

BEGINNING THE INITIATION

Katelyn McCarthy being Baptized by Father Carl McCarthy at St. Elizabeth Church in Curdsville circa 1997. Father McCarthy is the infant's second cousin. *Submitted by Peggy McCarthy*

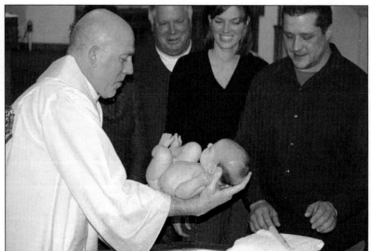

CLEANSED

SS. Joseph & Paul pastor Father Carl McCarthy is shown here baptizing Haden Marie Lehecka in November 2009. Also pictured are Pat Elder and Haden's parents Paul and Harmony Lehecka. *Submitted by April Dickens*

The First Sacrament

Father Eric Riley baptizes Lilian Grace Simon in 2010 at St. John the Baptist in Fordsville. Lilian is the daughter of Nastasia and Jason Simon.
Submitted by Margaret Montgomery

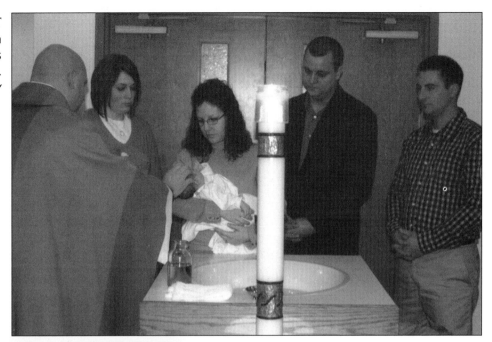

Easter Vigil

Sponsor Andrew Durham rests his hand on the right shoulder of Adam Yeisley as Father J. Patrick Reynolds pours water during the Sacrament of Baptism at the Easter Vigil on Saturday, April 3, 2010, at St. Thomas More in Paducah. Easter Vigil begins after sundown on Holy Saturday. The vigil is symbolic of waiting at the tomb of Jesus for His resurrection and a time of meditating on His death. The Easter Vigil service is also devoted to the Baptism of the Elect, who have spent the year receiving instruction from a catechist in the principles of the Catholic faith and now wish to officially enter the Church. *Photo by Stan Eckenberg*

9

First Communion
One of three Sacraments of Christian Initiation

First Communion is the colloquial name for a person's first reception of the Sacrament of the Eucharist. Eucharist in the Catholic Church refers to both the consecrated bread and wine and the ceremony during which it is consecrated. Once the bread and wine are consecrated, they become the actual Body and Blood of Christ. While the appearance of the elements does not change, the reality does.

Once consecrated, the bread and wine are known as the Blessed Sacrament and are treated with reverence and are typically stored in a locked stationary container called a tabernacle. The Blessed Sacrament is reserved to be used when visiting the sick or dying and as a focal point for the adoration of Jesus Christ, who is now present in the host.

Before receiving Communion for the first time, Catholic children complete an extended period of religious education. They must have sufficient knowledge and careful preparation so they understand the mystery of Christ and are able to receive the Eucharist with faith and devotion.

Because the Eucharist is central to the life of a Catholic, receiving it for the first time is a significant occasion for family celebration. Communicants wear special clothing, with girls typically wearing fancy white dresses with veils purchased for the occasion or handed down from a family member.

Jesus said to them, "Amen, amen, I say to you, unless you eat the flesh of the Son of Man and drink his blood, you do not have life within you. Whoever eats my flesh and drinks my blood has eternal life, and I will raise him on the last day. For my flesh is true food, and my blood is true drink. Whoever eats my flesh and drinks my blood remains in me and I in him. Just as the living Father sent me and I have life because of the Father, so also the one who feeds on me will have life because of me. This is the bread that came down from heaven. Unlike your ancestors who ate and still died, whoever eats this bread will live forever."

John 6: 53-58

Soul of Christ, sanctify me. Body of Christ, save me. Blood of Christ, inebriate me. Water from the side of Christ, wash me. Passion of Christ, strengthen me. O good Jesus hear me. Within Your wounds hide me. Separated from You, let me never be. From the evil one protect me. At the hour of my death, call me. And bid me come to You. That with Your saints, I may be praising You forever and ever. Amen.

The Anima Christi

St. Mary of the Woods

A First Communion class circa 1936 at St. Mary of the Woods parish in Whitesville. Front row, left to right: Damian Wright, Dennie Sapp, W.A. Howard, Victor Wilkerson, Charles Wedding, Marvin Boarman, Robert Clark and Carl Mills. Second row, left to right: Rita Barrett, Katie Boarman, Ita Belle Howard, an unknown girl, Lucille Mills, Margaret Phillips, Mary Catherine Basham and Pauline Dickens. Third row, left to right: Christine Mayfield, Martha Rose Howard, Mary Anna Mattingly, Christine Edge, Martha Rose Wilkerson, Josephine Jones, Mildred Edge and an unknown girl. Fourth row, left to right: Joe Howard, Wes Mosley, J.C. Hardesty, Howard Basham, Tommy Conder, Cliff Mills, Kenneth Westerfield, Tommy Hagan, Jimmy Ward and Red Mosley. Back row, left to right: Three unknown boys and Jacob Jones.
Submitted by the Arnold Howard Family

Future Bishop

Young Henry J. Soenneker on his First Communion Day at St. Boniface Church in Melrose, Minn. Henry Soenneker was born on May 27, 1907 and ordained to the priesthood on May 26, 1934. He was appointed the second bishop of the Diocese of Owensboro on March 15, 1961, his Episcopal Ordination was April 26, 1961, and he was installed as Bishop on May 9, 1961. Bishop Soenneker retired in 1982 and passed away on Sept. 24, 1987.
Submitted by Diocesan Archives

First Eucharist

The 1942 First Communion class of Holy Guardian Angels Parish, Irvington. *Submitted by Holy Guardian Angels Parish*

Committee of Catholic Chaplains in charge of arrangements for Solemn Pontifical Field Mass, Mother's Day, May 9, 1943, Camp Campbell, Ky.

Seated: Ch. (Major) Eugene P. Walsh.
Standing; (left to right) Ch. (1st. Lt.) Aloysius C. Zielinski; Cg. (Capt.) Lloyd C. Fortin; Ch. (Capt.) Theodore C. Pawlowiez; Ch. (Capt.) Stephen P. Kenny; Ch. (1st Lt.) William Facciuto; Ch. (1st Lt.) Gabriel H. Gianascol.

Submitted by Diocesan Archives

Field Mass

Soldiers at Camp Campbell near Hopkinsville receive Communion during a Solemn Pontifical Field Mass featuring Bishop Francis R. Cotton on Mother's Day, May 9, 1943. *Submitted by Diocesan Archives*

All Dressed Up

Pat Fulkerson is dressed up and ready for his First Holy Communion at a parish in Daviess County in May 1944. *Submitted by Bob and Ann Mattingly*

First Eucharist

Sister Jovita Milner, O.S.U., and Father John J. Glenn with the First Communion class of 1946 at St. Elizabeth parish in Curdsville. Front row, left to right: Ted Greenwell, J.D. Mahoney, Tony Wall, Nancy Murphy, Martha Calhoun, Patsy Calhoun, Tom Murphy, Tony Payne and George Kaufield. Back row, left to right: Martin Joe Frakes, Robbie Wall, Jo Ann Payne, Patty Mahoney, Eleanor Clements, Joan Payne and Peggy Murphy. St. Elizabeth Church was dedicated on Dec. 11, 1887 with first resident pastor, Father Joseph Wright, arriving in 1910. *Submitted by Peggy McCarthy*

BLESSED SACRAMENT PARISH

Blessed Sacrament Chapel's First Communion class of 1945. The black Catholic Community of Owensboro gathered together as a congregation to meet at Blessed Sacrament Chapel, a mission church of St. Stephen Cathedral Parish with St. Stephen priests ministering to the congregation. This photo includes Father Robert Connor, who helped establish a school and church in Owensboro for black Catholics. *Submitted by Veronica Wilhite*

STAR PUPILS

The SS. Joseph & Paul School, Owensboro, First Communion class sits in the classroom on May 17, 1952. *Submitted by Ruth Ann Carrico*

14

CORPUS CHRISTI

Bishop Francis R. Cotton presiding at Benediction during the diocesan-wide Corpus Christi procession at Mount Saint Joseph in 1956. The Corpus Christi procession is a historical tradition dating back to the 14th century and has been celebrated every year since the Diocese of Owensboro was established in 1937. *Submitted by Diocesan Archives*

First Communion

The First Communion class of 1958 with Father Maurice Tiell, pastor of Blessed Sacrament Chapel in Owensboro.
Submitted by Veronica Wilhite

Cathedral Class

The St. Stephen Cathedral First Communion class on the Cathedral steps on May 10, 1959.
Graphic Art Studio photo by Robert D. Chambers, submitted by Pam Huff and St. Stephen Cathedral

Class of 1960

The First Communion Class from Our Lady of Lourdes Church in Owensboro posed on October 16, 1960, with pastor Father Victor Boarman on the altar steps in front of the tabernacle.
Submitted by Our Lady of Lourdes Parish

New Communicants

Smiling children who just received their First Holy Communion gather for a group photo in May 1967, on the front steps of St. Mary Catholic Church in Franklin. The church was built in 1953 under the pastorate of Father Robert Healy of the Glenmary Home Missioners. Front row, left to right, First Communicants Stephanie Wilwayco, Debbie Garrett, Jerry Wilhite and Jim Kelly. Middle row, left to right: First Communicants Johnny Estep, Tommy Ford, Timmy Rafferty and Joey Estep. Back row, left to right: Teacher Joann Bradford and St. Mary pastor, Father Gus Guppenberger of the Glenrnary Home Missioners. The three people at top left are unidentified.
Submitted by St. Mary Parish Archive

CLASS PICTURE
The St. Stephen Cathedral First Communion class portrait taken on May 7, 1961. *Arrow Studio photo submitted by Pam Huff and St. Stephen Cathedral*

MILESTONE
This May 6, 1962, photo shows the First Communion class on the front steps of St. Stephen Cathedral in Owensboro. *Submitted by Pam Huff and St. Stephen Cathedral*

THE CHALICE
The chalice and Paten from St. Stephen Cathedral in Owensboro. A chalice is a standing cup used to hold sacramental wine during the Eucharist. Chalices are often made of precious metal, and they are sometimes richly embelished and jewelled. *Submitted by Diocesan Archives*

TABERNACLE

The Catholic Church teaches the doctrine of transubstantiation – that Christ is truly present, Body and Blood, Soul and Divinity – though under the appearance of bread and/or wine. This presence continues after consecration, so even after Mass is concluded, the Eucharistic elements are still Christ's Body and Blood. A tabernacle serves as a secure place in which to store the Blessed Sacrament before carrying to the sick who cannot participate in Mass or to serve as a focal point for the prayers of those who visit the church. Some tabernacles are veiled when the Eucharist is present within. These veils are often of cloth and design similar to the priest's vestments, and are either white, gold, violet, green or red depending on the liturgical color of the day or season. Tabernacles have generally been made of metal or sometimes of heavy wood. They are traditionally lined in white cloth, and are always securely locked and affixed or bolted to their support.

Submitted by Diocesan Archives

READY FOR COMMUNION

The First Communion Class of 1963 at St. Stephen Cathedral in Owensboro.
Submitted by Pam Huff and St. Stephen Cathedral

THEIR SPECIAL DAY

The specific year of this First Communion class photo from St. Stephen School in Owensboro is unknown, but it was probably taken during the late 1960s. *Arrow Studio photo submitted by Pam Huff and St. Stephen Cathedral*

1964 CLASS

St. Stephen Cathedral First Communion class in 1964.
Arrow Studio photo submitted by Pam Huff and St. Stephen Cathedral

IN REMEMBRANCE

Mike McCarthy stands with Father Frank Howard and Sister Helen Ann Stuart, O.S.U., at St. Elizabeth Church in Curdsville. The photo was taken in May 1972 after Mike McCarthy received his First Communion.
Submitted by Peggy McCarthy

THE LORD'S SUPPER

Monsignor George Hancock and Sister Helen Ann Stuart, O.S.U., with the First Communion class of 1974 at St. Elizabeth Church in Curdsville. The class received their First Eucharist on May 12, 1974.
Submitted by Peggy McCarthy

OUR LADY OF THE SNOWS

Owensboro Bishop John J. McRaith speaks with Keith Franey and Jeff Cooke after a Mass at Our Lady of the Snows Shrine in Belleville, Ill., in May 1984.
Submitted by Diocesan Archives

REVERENTIAL RESPECT

Father Joseph Rhodes posed with the First Communion Class from St. Stephen Cathedral on April 20, 1980.
Submitted by Pam Huff and St. Stephen Cathedral

BLESS THE CHILD
Bishop John J. McRaith lays hands on a child's head to offer a blessing on Aug. 11, 1985. During Mass, the priest offers a blessing instead of Communion for children and adults who are not yet eligible to receive the Eucharist.
Submitted by Diocesan Archives

MARKING LENT
The late Father Danny Goff, chairperson of the religion department at Owensboro Catholic High School during his career there, puts the finishing touches on a wooden cross placed in the school's courtyard for Lent. Watching, left to right, are students David Johnson and Richard Hayden who helped him erect the cross. *Photo by Steve Rocco*

REMEMBERING THE PASSION

The entire faculty and student body from Trinity High School in Whitesville marched with other members of the community in the 1987 Good Friday Procession in Owensboro. The march is held each year in remembrance of Jesus' passion and death. *Western Kentucky Catholic photo by Mel Howard*

ST. JOHN THE BAPTIST

Glenmary Father Joe O'Donnell administers First Communion during the 1980s at St. John the Baptist Church in Fordsville. Father O'Donnell retired in 1996. *Submitted by Margaret Montgomery*

PICNIC AT MT. ST. JOSEPH

The Steve Hollman family from St. Pius X parish in Owensboro enjoys a meal at the Maple Mount picnic in 1994. *Western Kentucky Catholic photo by Mel Howard*

EUCHARISTIC PRAYER
The Eucharistic prayer during a Mass celebrating the 175th anniversary of St. Lawrence Church in St. Lawrence on Aug. 10, 1997.
Submitted by Diocesan Archives

FATHER BRADLEY
Father Ed Bradley elevates the cup at a Sunday Mass at Holy Name of Jesus Church in Henderson in 1998. *Western Kentucky Catholic photo by Mel Howard*

ST. MARK
Shirley Keeney places a Host into the ciborium as Mr. and Mrs. Ernie Davis look on at St. Mark Church in Eddyville on March 28, 1999. It is a Catholic custom in smaller chapels and churches for members of the assembly to place a host in the ciborium if they wish to receive communion.
Submitted by Diocesan Archives

Prayerfully Received

Cassie Thomas received her First Communion from Father Richard Powers at St. Mary Magdalene Church in Owensboro on April 30, 2005.
Submitted by Peggy McCarthy

Body of Christ

Kelsey McCarthy receives her First Communion from Father Richard Powers at St. Elizabeth Church in Curdsville on May 13, 2006.
Submitted by Peggy McCarthy

Invitation

Men of St. John the Baptist Church in Fordsville portray the Last Supper on their float for the local Christmas parade on Dec. 11, 2004.
Submitted by Margaret Montgomery

Motorized Celebration

After her First Communion at Precious Blood Parish in Owensboro on April 26, 2009, Lydea Dickens poses for a different kind of commemorative photo with her Grandpa Leo Dickens on his motorcycle. Also pictured are her brothers Luke and Lance Dickens. *Submitted by April Dickens*

Easter Vigil Celebration

The Rite of Christian Initiation of Adults (RCIA) prepared eleven to be welcomed into St. Thomas More Church in Paducah during the 2010 Easter Vigil. They received the Sacraments of Initiation including Baptism with water, Confirmation with Chrism oil, Communion with the Body and Blood of Jesus in the form of bread and wine, and were then sent forth to love and serve the Lord. The newly received then participate in instruction for a period of up to one year which seeks to deepen spiritual growth through instruction about living the Catholic faith and incorporation into parish life. Their neophyte – a term used to describe new converts – year will culminate on the anniversary of initiation, the next Easter. Sponsors play a special role in the RCIA process, acting as a companion with the participant through the spiritual journey to provide assistance and guidance. From the beginning of the RCIA process they join in the preparation classes, answer questions, are present as the participants are welcomed into full Communion with the Church, and may continue a lifelong relationship with those they sponsor. First row, left to right: Adam Yeisley (baptized), Andrew Durham (sponsor), Teresa Elliott (godparent), Sara Neihoff (baptized), Eric Neihoff (baptized), Duane Neihoff (godparent), Jonna Neihoff, Jonathan Neihoff (sponsor). Second row, left to right: Angela Yeisley, Robert Browning, Jeremy Childers, Randy Newcomb, Kevin Segebarth, Annie Segebarth, Laurie Straub. Third row, left to right: Delores Webber (sponsor), Randy Froehlich (sponsor), Ernie Mitchell (sponsor), Terry Larbes (sponsor), Michael Chesnut (RCIA Director and sponsor), Eileen Segebarth (sponsor), Kelli Walk (sponsor). Back row, left to right: Father Daniel Dillard and Father Pat Reynolds. *Photo by Stan Eckenberg*

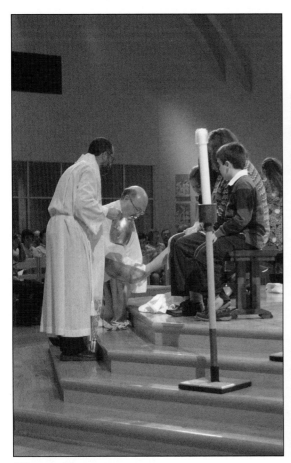

HOLY THURSDAY

Concelebrant Father Lázero Rentería, left, assists Father J. Patrick Reynolds in washing the foot of Alyssa Todino during the Holy Thursday Mass on April 1, 2010, at St. Thomas More Church in Paducah. This was a bilingual evening Mass of the Lord's Supper which was the first of three services of the Paschal Triduum during Holy Week. Holy Thursday celebrates the institution of the Eucharist and priesthood.
Photo by Stan Eckenberg

GOOD FRIDAY

Server Taylor Mudd, left, and seminarian Joseph Markin bring forth the candle as server Michael Langston venerates the cross and server Flynn Mudd and Father Daniel Dillard look on at St. Thomas More Church in Paducah on Good Friday, July 2, 2010. Good Friday is Friday during Holy Week, and is traditionally a time of fasting and penance, a solemn commemoration of Christ's passion, crucifixion and death. For Christians, Good Friday commemorates not just an historical event, but the sacrificial death of Christ which, with His life and resurrection, comprises the heart of the Christian faith.
Photo by Stan Eckenberg

BISHOP'S BLESSING
Bishop William Medley blesses first grade student Molly Bennett during Holy Communion at an all-school Mass at SS. Peter & Paul Church in Hopkinsville on Wednesday, March 31, 2010. This visit to SS. Peter & Paul was the second of three visits by Bishop Medley to the parish in a two-week period. *Photo by Dawn C. Ligibel*

ST. FRANCIS BORGIA
Father Larry McBride is shown consecrating the Eucharist for Holy Communion at St. Francis Borgia in Sturgis. Father McBride became the pastor for three different Parishes – St. Francis Borgia in Sturgis, St. Ambrose in Henshaw and St. William in Marion – in June 2005. Father McBride quickly became a joy and blessing to all three communities.
Photo submitted by St. Francis Borgia Parish

Confirmation
One of Three Sacraments of Christian Initiation

The Sacrament of Confirmation is one of the Sacraments of Christian Initiation. It marks an important milestone in the faith formation of a Catholic. Once all three sacraments – Baptism, Confirmation and Eucharist – are received, the individual is considered a fully initiated member of the church.

As with First Eucharist, there is a preparation period prior to the reception of Confirmation. This is an opportunity for further education in the teachings of the Church and the lifestyle of a Catholic. In the Diocese of Owensboro, the bishop has set the age of Confirmation to be at least 7th grade. The sacrament is conferred on individuals who have properly and reasonably requested it. By doing this, the Holy Spirit is invited into their body to strengthen and fortify them in their faith. According to the Catechism of the Catholic Church, "by the sacrament of Confirmation, [the baptized] are more perfectly bound to the Church and are enriched with a special strength of the Holy Spirit. Hence they are, as true witnesses of Christ, more strictly obliged to spread and defend the faith by word and deed."

Now when the apostles in Jerusalem heard that Samaria had accepted the word of God, they sent them Peter and John, who went down and prayed for them, that they might receive the holy Spirit, for it had not yet fallen upon any of them; they had only been baptized in the name of the Lord Jesus. Then they laid hands on them and they received the holy Spirit.
Acts 8:14-17

I believe in God, the Father almighty, creator of heaven and earth, and in Jesus Christ, his only Son, our Lord, who was conceived by the Holy Spirit, born of the Virgin Mary, suffered under Pontius Pilate, was crucified, died, and was buried. He descended into hell; the third day he rose again from the dead; he ascended into heaven and is seated at the right hand of the Father; from thence he shall come to judge the living and the dead. I believe in the Holy Spirit, the holy Catholic Church, the Communion of Saints, the forgiveness of sins, the resurrection of the body, and life everlasting. Amen.
The Apostles' Creed

Confirmed
Bishop John J. McRaith administers the Sacrament of Confirmation at a Mass at Rosary Chapel in Paducah in June 1993.
Submitted by Diocesan Archives

On Base
Bishop John J. McRaith, back center, with confirmandi and witnesses at The U.S. Army Armor Center in Fort Knox in 2003.
Submitted by Diocesan Archives

CONFIRMANDI
Confirmation at Holy Guardian Angels Parish, Irvington, on May 26, 2010, was one of the first Confirmations celebrated in the Diocese by the fourth Bishop of Owensboro, William F. Medley. Also pictured is Holy Guardian Angels pastor Father Greg Trawick with the four young people who received the Sacrament of Confirmation. *Submitted by Holy Guardian Angels Parish*

Reconciliation
A Reconciliation with God Through Confession of Sins and Offering of Penance

The Sacrament of Reconciliation is also known by many Catholics as "Penance" or "Confession." In reality it includes all three of those elements. The sacrament begins with the private confession of sins to a priest or Confessor. To truly receive the benefit of the sacrament, the Penitent must feel sincere sorrow for the acts confessed. Next, the Penitent offers prayers of repentance while the priest asks God's forgiveness on their behalf. Finally, the Penitent is reconciled with God and the Church when the priest – as an ordained minister of Christ – offers absolution or forgiveness on behalf of God and the Church.

The Sacrament of Penance is necessary because the cleansing of the soul during Baptism only washes away sins committed previously. After Baptism, we must periodically reconcile ourselves with God and the Church by confessing and repenting of any mortal or serious sin we may have committed. Catholics must be reconciled with God for all but venial sins in order to be worthy to receive Communion. For that reason, the first confession is usually made between the Sacraments of Baptism and First Eucharist.

For Catholic priests, the confidentiality of all statements made by Penitents during the course of confession is absolute. This strict confidentiality is known as the "Seal of the Confessional" and is mandated by Canon Law and recognized in civil law.

> Therefore whoever eats the bread or drinks the cup of the Lord unworthily will have to answer for the body and blood of the Lord. A person should examine himself, and so eat the bread and drink the cup. For anyone who eats and drinks without discerning the body, eats and drinks judgment on himself.
>
> *1 Corinthians 11:27-29*

O my God, I am heartily sorry for having offended Thee and I detest all my sins, because I dread the loss of heaven and the pains of hell, but most of all because they offend Thee, my God, who are all good and deserving of all my love. I firmly resolve, with the help of Thy grace, to confess my sins, to do penance, and to amend my life.

Act of Contrition

RECONCILIATION AND RENEWAL

A Reconciliation and Renewal Mass at the Owensboro Sportscenter led by Bishop Cotton circa 1958. Bishop Charles Herman Helmsing of the new Springfield-Cape Girardeau, Mo., Diocese was a guest speaker at the event.
McFarland Photography photo submitted by Diocesan Archives

First Reconciliation Day

After their First Reconciliation, these children celebrate with a party in the basement at St. Mary Parish in Franklin on Feb. 27, 1966. The small basement was a fellowship hall and CCD classroom from 1953 until a 9,700-square-foot building expansion project was completed in 1999. Father Raymond Berthiaume stands with penitents, left to right, Steven Bradford, Larry Jasinski, Jim Wilkerson, Charmane Fowler, Linda Wilkerson and Terri Stoll.
Submitted by St. Mary Parish Archive

Reconciled

Bishop Soenneker leads a Diocesan Reconciliation Mass in 1976 at the Sportscenter in Owensboro.
Submitted by Diocesan Archives

Tree of Renewal

Jan Howard, president of the parish council for Precious Blood parish in Owensboro, holds the parishes' RENEW tree at the kick off Mass at the Owensboro Sportscenter in 1985. He is with Father Bob Willett; Sister Barbara Peterson, S.C.N., parish RENEW coordinator; Keith Franey and Larry McBride.
Western Kentucky Catholic photo by K.C. Meadows

SINGING FOR RENEWAL
Sister Cheryl Clemons, O.S.U., and Sister Stephanie
Warren, O.S.U., provide music at a RENEW event in 1985.
Western Kentucky Catholic photo by Mel Howard

RENEW 2000
RENEW 2000 director Sister Pat Froning, O.S.F., speaks
with Sister Kathy Warren, right, from the RENEW
International team at a conference on Sept. 27, 1997.
Submitted by Diocesan Archives

Reconciliation

Father Ben Luther, left, and Father Richard Cash, right, hear the confessions of two young Catholics in the Brescia University gym during the Youth 2000 Eucharistic Retreat on March 7, 2010. For a Catholic, confessing one's sins to a Catholic priest and receiving absolution for having committed those sins places one's soul in a state of grace – which is necessary to worthily receive the Body and Blood of Christ during Mass. In recent times, priests report, many Catholics do not receive the Sacrament of Reconciliation frequently except perhaps to fulfill one's "Easter Duty." The Catholic Church requires that all Catholics who have made their First Communion receive the Holy Eucharist sometime during the Easter season, which lasts through Pentecost Sunday, 50 days after Easter. If they have committed a serious sin, Catholics must also take part in the Sacrament of Reconciliation before receiving this Easter communion. *Submitted by Mel Howard*

BLESSINGS FOR THE PENITENT
During Summer Camp L.I.F.E. 2 in 2009, at Gasper River Catholic Youth Camp and Retreat Center, Father Frank Ruff blesses a penitent after hearing the admission of sins. He offers the church's absolution from sin, and assigns a penance to be performed as an act of sorrow for sin and to strengthen the penitent's resolve to sin no more. *Photo by Susan Warrell, submitted by Diocesan Archives*

GASPER RIVER YOUTH CAMP AND RETREAT CENTER
Bishop John J. McRaith with a penitent at Gasper River Catholic Youth Camp and Retreat Center Summer Camp L.I.F.E. 2 in 2009. *Photo by Susan Warrell, submitted by Diocesan Archives*

Returning One's Soul to a State of Sanctifying Grace

Father Ben Luther, at back, listened to a young Franciscan Friar from New York who was part of the mission team of priests who preached the Youth 2000 Eucharistic Retreat in the Brescia University Gym on March 7, 2010. This scene illustrates the Catholic Church's belief about the Sacrament of Reconciliation: Father Ben as the confessor hears the penitent's self-accusations of sins, weighs the sincerity of the penitent's contrition and resolve to sin no more, and offers to the penitent the Church's absolution from sin, returning the penitent's soul to a state of sanctifying grace, a supernatural gift of God to intellectual creatures (men, angels) for their eternal salvation. The confessor then gives the penitent a penance to peform to begin the process of atoning to God and the Church for one's sins with a firm resolve not to commit them again. *Submitted by Mel Howard*

Receiving Absolution

Father Jerry Riney, pastor of Holy Spirit Church, Bowling Green, heard confessions at the Gasper River Catholic Youth Camp and Retreat Center Summer Camp L.I.F.E. 1 in 2009. This picture illustrates the moment of absolution from sin when the confessor prays with the penitent that their confessed sins may be absolved from their soul. *Photo by Susan Warrell, submitted by Diocesan Archives*

RECONCILIATION BEFORE THE BLESSED SACRAMENT

A young woman and a Franciscan Friar pray before the Blessed Sacrament contained within a monstrance atop a pyramid of lights in the center of Brescia University's gym during the March 7, 2010 Youth 2000 Retreat. Catholics often perform their penance received during the Sacrament of Reconciliation by praying in a church before the Blessed Sacrament – who is Jesus really present in the host inside the monstrance. A penance need not be a painful experience, but an act of prayer or sacrifice, often both, offered to God in atonement for sins committed, and to strengthen the penitent's resolve not to commit sin again.
Submitted by Mel Howard

Holy Orders
Men Ordained to Offer the Sacraments

There are three levels of Holy Orders which a Catholic man may receive. The first level of orders is to the diaconate. There are two types – transitional and permanent – of deacons. Transitional deacons are typically on the path to priesthood, but are not necessarily required to be. Deacons are ministers of service and are empowered to act in the name of the Church to offer the Sacrament of Baptism, witness the Sacrament of Marriage, preach and be advocates of social justice.

The Sacrament of Holy Orders makes an indelible mark on the soul, and that mark is only made one time. When a Deacon moves to the Priesthood, it is an extension of the original sacrament already received. Through invocation of the Holy Spirit, the new priest is now empowered to offer any sacrament except the Sacrament of Holy Orders. A priest elevated to the level of Bishop, may offer all of the sacraments including that of Holy Orders through additional strength from the Holy Spirit.

Then Jesus approached and said to them, "All power in heaven and on earth has been given to me. Go, therefore, and make disciples of all nations, baptizing them in the name of the Father, and of the Son, and of the holy Spirit, teaching them to observe all that I have commanded you. And behold, I am with you always, until the end of the age."

Matthew 28:18-20

O God, Who hast appointed Thine only-begotten Son to be the eternal High Priest for the glory of Thy Majesty and the salvation of mankind; grant that they whom He hath chosen to be His ministers and the stewards of His Mysteries, may be found faithful in the fulfillment of the ministry which they have received. Through the same Christ our Lord. Amen.

A Prayer for Priests

FAMILY PORTRAIT

Anna Spalding Lanham, left, with her older brother
Father Louis Spalding, son-in-law Edward Kelly and
daughter Edwina Lanham Kelly on the steps of St.
Angela Hall at Mount St. Joseph. Father Spalding
was ordained in 1887 and served as pastor of St.
William parish in Knottsville for 20 years and later
as chaplain at Mount St. Joseph. Father Spalding
passed away in 1920, before the Diocese of
Owensboro was formed.
Submitted by the Arnold Howard Family

MINOR SEMINARY

A young Francis R. Cotton is among these students
in minor seminary. He was born on Sept. 19, 1895. His
ordination to the priesthood was June 17, 1920. He was
appointed the first Bishop of the Diocese of Owensboro
on Dec. 16, 1937, had his Episcopal Ordination on Feb.
24, 1938 and was installed as Bishop on March 8, 1938.
Bishop Cotton passed away on Sept. 25, 1960.
Submitted by Diocesan Archives

SEMINARIANS
Francis R. Cotton, right, with fellow seminarians at school sometime prior to his ordination to the priesthood which occured on June 17, 1920. *Submitted by Diocesan Archives*

ORDINATION OF DEACONS
Francis R. Cotton (marked with an arrow) is among this group of candidates for the diaconate on May 24, 1920. Candidates prostrate themselves during a portion of the ritual of ordination of deacons while the Bishop and clergy recite the Litany of the Saints. *Submitted by Diocesan Archives*

Early Pastors

A composite of three early pastors of St. William Church in Knottsville. Father James P. Cronin, right, was the first pastor of St. William and served from 1887 to 1892. Father Louis H. Spalding, left, served as pastor from 1893 to 1914. Father Francis J. Timoney was pastor from 1915 to 1920. None of these priests were living to see the formation of the Diocese of Owensboro in 1937. *Photo by Choitzer Studio, submitted by Millie Carrico*

Seminary Days

Francis R. Cotton during his seminary days.
Submitted by Diocesan Archives

On the Go

Father George Niehaus in his car at St. Lawrence parish in St. Lawrence during the 1920s when the area was still part of the Diocese of Louisville. Father Niehaus was pastor at St. Lawrence from 1914 to 1931. He was ordained on Dec. 18, 1885 and passed away in 1932.
Submitted by Ruth Ann Carrico

BUILDER

Pastor of Holy Guardian Angels Parish Father Jerome Hoepf, C.PP.S., oversaw the construction of the Parish's new church building in Irvington to replace the 75-year-old structure in Mount Merino during the early 1930s. He is shown here standing on the steps of the new parish church which was dedicated on Oct. 30, 1933. *Submitted by Holy Guardian Angels Parish.*

YOUNG SEMINARIAN

Father Henry Joseph Soenneker at the time of his ordination to the priesthood. He studied at Ponifical College Josephinum in Columbus, Ohio, from 1921 until his ordination to the priesthood on May 26, 1934. *Submitted by Diocesan Archives*

CELEBRATION

Newly ordained Bishop Francis R. Cotton, stands outside St. Stephen Cathedral in Owensboro with priests and others after his ordination mass on Dec. 16, 1937. He served as the first Bishop of the newly formed Diocese of Owensboro, formerly part of what became the Archdiocese of Louisville. *Submitted by Diocesan Archives*

Raising the First Bishop
The ordination of Bishop Francis R. Cotton, the first bishop of the Diocese of Owensboro, took place at St. Stephen Cathedral in Owensboro on Dec. 16, 1937. Bishop Cotton is seated at left facing the altar. *Submitted by Diocesan Archives*

NEWLY ORDAINED

Charles Thomas Libs was ordained into the priesthood on June 3, 1939, at the age of 26. Father Libs was the pastor at St. Anthony Church in Utica and helped found St. Sebastian Church in Calhoun. *Submitted by Bob and Ann Mattingly*

GATHERING

Father Charles Thomas Libs of Daviess County, second from left, with unknown priests probably during the 1940s. *Submitted by Bob and Ann Mattingly*

FATHER EGAN

Father Joseph J. Egan was pastor of St. William and St. Lawrence Churches from 1938 to 1942. He was ordained on May 30, 1931 and entered the Congregation of the Passionists in 1941, where he received the religious name of Father Declan Egan, C.P. Father Egan passed away on June 26, 1992 at the age of 87. *Submitted by Millie Carrico*

THE APOSTLE'S TOMB

Father Charles Thomas Libs of Daviess County, front row fourth from left, poses with other priests inside St. Peter's Basilica in Rome probably during the 1940s. St. Peter's is a Late Renaissance church located inside Vatican City. It has the largest interior of any Christian church in the world and can accommodate 60,000 people. Tradition holds that St. Peter's Basilica is the burial site of St. Peter, one of Jesus' apostles and the first Bishop of Rome. His tomb is located directly below the altar.
Submitted by Bob and Ann Mattingly

SILVER ANNIVERSARY

The silver anniversary of the ordination of Father John C. Hallahan (in white chasuble in center of steps) in 1955 was held at St. William Church in Knottsville. Altar servers, women of the parish who helped organize the celebration, and brother priests are pictured here. *Submitted by Father Joe Mills*

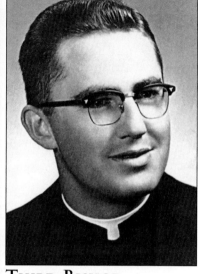

THIRD BISHOP
John Jeremiah McRaith was born on Dec. 6, 1934 and ordained to the priesthood on Feb. 21, 1960. He was ordained Bishop of the Diocese of Owensboro on Dec. 15, 1982, and retired in January 2009.
Submitted by Diocesan Archives

FULFILLING OBLIGATIONS
Bishop Francis R. Cotton at his ad limina visit to Pope John XXIII in Rome in 1959. The Decree of the Consistorial Congregation, issued by order of Pope Pius X in 1909 states that every bishop must render to the pope an account of the state of his diocese once every five years. Bishops, when they come to Rome in fulfilment of their obligation of ad limina, must also visit the tombs of the apostles. These quinquennial periods began in 1911 and Bishops from the Americas report in the fourth year of each period. *Submitted by Diocesan Archives*

ALL ARE ONE IN CHRIST

Newly consecrated Bishop Henry Joseph Soenneker with his Bishop Consecrator and co-Consecrators after the ceremony at St. Mary Cathedral in St. Cloud, Minn., on April 26, 1961. When he was consecrated, he took as his motto, "All Are One In Christ." He was installed as the second Bishop of the Diocese of Owensboro on May 9, 1961, at a ceremony at St. Stephen Cathedral.
Submitted by Diocesan Archives

Bishop's Coat-of-Arms Tells History Of Owensboro Diocese, His Family

The coat-of-arms of Most Rev. Henry J. Soenneker like all episcopal heraldry tells a great deal about his diocese and his family background.

The surmounting hat is in the episcopal color, green, with six tassels on a side, denoting the rank of a bishop. The single bar of the cross beneath the hat, with the mitre and crozier also denote the rank of a bishop.

The left field denotes his jurisdiction, namely the Diocese of Owensboro, Ky. The martyr's palm between two stones represents Saint Stephen, the Protomartyr, the titular of the Cathedral of Owensboro. "Full of faith (represented by the cross dividing the main partition of the shield) and the Holy Ghost," he was chosen by the Apostles as the first of the seven deacons (Acts 6:1-5). Stoned to death at the instigation of the Sanhedrin, he became the first Christian martyr. His dying prayer obtained the conversion of Saint Paul, who was actively engaged in his martyrdom.

The chief (upper partition) bears two clasped hands derived from the seal of Kentucky to represent the great State in which the Diocese of Owensboro is located. The State seal manifests two gentlemen, with two hands clasped and the other two resting on each other's shoulders, standing above a scroll bearing the motto, "United we stand, divided we fall." According to the Kentucky State Historical Society, Isaac Shelby, the first Governor of the State, probably suggested the motto complementing the clasped hands of the seal.

The right field denotes the personal coat-of-arms of Bishop Soenneker. Joined as it is, to the diocesan arms, it signifies the wedding of a Bishop to his See, a thought also expressed by the episcopal ring worn by the Bishop on his right hand.

These personal arms are an "assumption" based on the etymology of the Bishop's surname. Many families bearing names with the root "Sonn" or "Sonne" display a sun in their coat of arms. Accordingly, a golden sun has been emblazoned in the base of the shield, on a green field reminiscent of the fertile plains in the Diocese of St. Cloud, where Bishop Soenneker was Spiritual Director of Saint John's Seminary of the Diocese at Collegeville at the time of his appointment to the episcopacy.

One of the stars in chief prays the patronage of the Blessed Virgin under her title "Star of the Sea," as the ever present guide to spiritual mariners, especially the Bishops, who are the Successors of the Apostles. The other represents the State of Minnesota, whose seal is inscribed with the legend "L'Etoile de Nord (Star of the North)," a reference to Minnesota's geographical position among the States, until the admission of Alaska to that Union on January 3, 1959. It was in this State of Minnesota that the Bishop was born, educated and labored as a priest prior to his episcopal consecration.

Henry II of Bavaria, Saint and King, and the husband of St. Cunegunda, is honored on the

OMNES UNUM IN CHRISTO

shield as the baptismal patron of Bishop Soenneker. The coat of arms of Bavaria, consisting of a field of silver and blue fusils (diamond-shaped objects), is abbreviated in the form of a fess (horizontal band), and charged with a golden crown as a symbol for St. Henry.

The Bishop's motto, **Omnes Unum in Christo**, means "All Are One in Christ." The motto is taken from Chapter 3, verse 28 of Saint Paul's letter to the Galatians: "There is neither Jew nor Greek; there is neither slave nor freeman; there is neither male nor female. For you are all one in Christ Jesus."

The external ornaments are composed of the pontifical hat with its six tassels on each side disposed in three rows, all in green, and the precious mitre, the processional cross and the crosier, all in gold. These are the presently accepted heraldic trappings of a prelate of the rank of Bishop. Before 1870, the pontifical hat was worn at solemn cavalcades held in conjunction with papal functions. The color of the pontifical hat and the number and color of the tassels were signs of the rank of a prelate, a custom which is still preserved in ecclesiastical heraldry.

Bishop Soenneker's coat-of-arms was designed from the firm of William F. J. Ryan of New York City.

SHARING HIS GIFT
Seminarian Lew White entertains fellow students with his guitar at St. Maur Seminary in South Union in 1966. White was ordained for a brief time before he died in a car accident on his way to Mass in December 1969. *Submitted by Father Mel Bennett*

VISITA AD LIMINA
Bishop Henry J. Soenneker's ad limina visit with Pope Paul VI in Rome. Bishop Soenneker had three ad limina visits with Paul VI during his leadership of the Diocese of Owensboro – in 1964, 1969 and 1974. The Pope passed away in 1978. *Submitted by Diocesan Archives*

FATHER YUNKER
Father Louis P. Yunker took up residence at St. John the Baptist in Fordsville after his retirement in 1971. At the time, the church did not have a full-time pastor. *Submitted by Margaret Montgomery*

Rev. Leonard Reisz   Rev. Bernard Powers   Rev. Joseph Mills   Rev. David Warren   Rev. Leonard Alvey

Rev. Ben Luther   Rev. Joseph J. Pilger   Rev. Louis F. Piskula   Rev. Maury D. Riney

Assistant Pastors

Rev. Leonard Reisz	1950
Rev Bernard A. Powers	1952
Rev. Joseph M. Mills	1953
Rev. David H. Warren	1956
Rev. Leonard Alvey	1958
Rev. Thomas A. Murphy	1958
Rev. Richard Powers	1959
Rev. Gerard Glahn	1959
Rev. Charles G. Fischer	1959
Rev. Thomas Clark	1955
Rev. Norbert C. Howard	1957
Rev. J. Francis Powers	1960
Rev. John J. Power	1962
Rev. Anthony Ziegler	1962
Rev. Gerald Calhoun	1964
Rev. John H. Nemmers	1965
Rev. Carl Asplund	1965
Rev. John Bartolomucce	1966
Rev. Clark G. Field	1967
Rev. Gerald Griffith	1968
Rev. Phillip I. Thomas	1969
Rev. Robert Willett	1969
Rev. Phillip Field	1970
Rev. Alan Pearson	1970

Rev. Thomas Murphy

Rev. Richard Powers

Rev. Charles Fischer

Rev. J. Francis Powers

Rev. Anthony Ziegler

Rev. Gerard Glahn

Rev. Thomas Clark

Rev. John J. Power

Rev. Gerald Calhoun   Rev. Clark G. Field   Rev. Gerald Griffith   Rev. Robert Willett   Rev. Phillip Field

Rev. Henry A. Cecil

Rev. Charles Richard Meredith

Assistant Pastors

Rev. Ben Luther	1969
Rev. Joseph J. Pilger	1971
Rev. Louis F. Piskula	1974
Rev. Henry A. Cecil	1976
Rev. Maury D. Riney	1977
Rev. Charles Richard Meredith	1978
Rev. J. Patrick Reynolds	1979
Rev. Henry Moman	1980
Rev. Anthony Stevenson	1981
Rev. Gerald H. Baker	1983
Rev. Anthony Bickett	1985
Rev. Kevin Karl	1987
Rev. Darrell Venters	1989

Rev. J. Patrick Reynolds

Rev. Henry Moman

Rev. Anthony Stevenson

Rev. Gerald H. Baker

Rev. Anthony Bickett   Rev. Kevin Karl   Rev. Darrell Venters

St. Stephen Priests

A composite record of priests serving as assistant pastor at St. Stephen Cathedral who began their assignment there between 1950 and 1989. *Submitted by Ruth Ann Carrico*

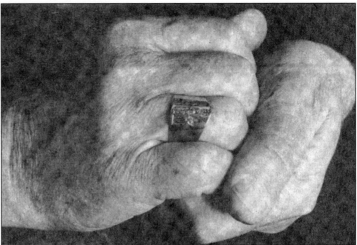

SPECIAL GIFT
Bishop Soenneker wore a ring he received from Pope John XXIII during the Vatican II Council in 1961. The ring has St. John and St. Peter on each side of Christ and the pope's seal in the underside. *Submitted by Diocesan Archives*

QUINQUENNIAL VISIT
Bishop Henry J. Soenneker's ad limina visit with Pope John Paul II in Rome in 1979. These required visits to the Pope and the tombs of the apostles occur every five years, and are properly called "quinquennial visita ad limina apostolorum." *Submitted by Diocesan Archives*

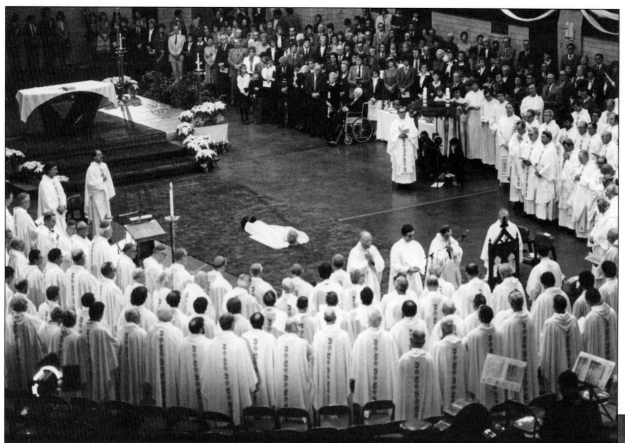

PROSTRATE BEFORE GOD

Surrounded by the priests of the diocese, Father John J. McRaith prostrates himself on the floor during a portion of the Mass in which he was ordained bishop of the Diocese of Owensboro. The ordination took place at the Owensboro Sportscenter on Dec. 15, 1982. *Submitted by Diocesan Archives*

NEIGHBORHOOD VISIT

Bishop John McRaith visits with two boys in the Rolling Heights neighborhood in Owensboro in 1985. According to the diocese, Bishops are routinely invited to meet with non-Catholics and they do so often. *Submitted by Judy Kapelsohn*

CHAPLAIN
Msgr. Gilbert Henninger, center left, a former Vicar General of the Diocese of Owensboro, sits with Father George Boehmicke during a Daughters of Isabella presentation at the Carmel Home in Owensboro during the 1980s. Father Boehmicke was the Daughters of Isabella chaplain for 25 years. *Submitted by the Daughters of Isabella*

GREEETINGS
When he was assigned at Christ The King Parish in Madisonville, this picture of Father John Meredith was taken after Mass one morning as he was holding Ella and Carla Whittington. Priests at Catholic parishes make it a custom to greet the people before and after weekend Masses. *Submitted by Christ The King Parish*

MINISTERING TO THE PEOPLE
Three priests who have ministered among the people of Christ The King Parish in Madisonville, from left, Father Jerry Glahn, Father Delma Clemons, and Father Jerry Baker. *Submitted by Christ The King Parish*

PAPAL VISIT

Bishop John J. McRaith makes his first quinquennial visit ad limina to Pope John Paul II in Rome in 1989. During this visit to report on the state of the diocese, Bishop McRaith would also have visited the tombs of the apostles, St. Peter and St. Paul.
Submitted by Diocesan Archives

PRECIOUS FATHERS

The Fathers of Precious Blood parish in Owensboro in 1986. Left to right: Father Carl Wise, Father Harold Diller, Father James McCabe, Father Henry Frantz and Father William Donahoe.
Western Kentucky Catholic photo

DEACONS

Four deacons stand in front of Immaculate Conception Church in Earlington on Feb. 18, 1995. The deacons, left to right: Stan Puryear, Mike Clark, Andy Ausenbaugh and Carl McCarthy. A deacon is an ordained minister of the Catholic Church. There are three groups, or "orders," of ordained ministers in the Church: bishops, presbyters and deacons. Deacons are ordained as a sacramental sign to the Church and to the world of Christ, who came "to serve and not to be served." The permanent diaconate is the only order of ordained ministers which will accept a married man if he has the support of his wife. A married permanent deacon may not move on to the priesthood and if he becomes a widower, he may not remarry and must remain celebate.
Submitted by Diocesan Archives

ORDINATION MASS

Rose Lowry from Rosary Chapel parish in Paducah leads the Black Catholic Commission Choir. They are joined by seminarians from St. Meinrad as they provide music for William Odom's diaconate ordination Mass on Feb. 9, 1991 in St. Stephen Cathedral.
Western Kentucky Catholic photo

Laying on of Hands

Father Jerry Calhoun lays hands on Deacon Mike Williams, while Father John Vaughn lays hands on Deacon Dave Kennedy during the RIte of Ordination to the priesthood in May 1997. During the Rite of Ordination, the officiant lays his hands upon the elect and calls upon the Holy Spirit. All priests present then lay their hands upon the elect as a sign of unity and encouragement.
Hubert Powers Photography photo submitted by Diocesan Archives

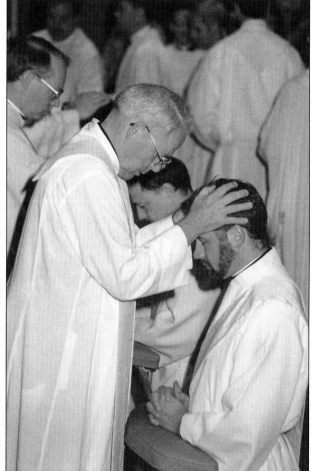

Personal Touch

Bishop John J. McRaith speaks with residents waiting in line for assistance at the Help Office of Owensboro. Bishop McRaith was always concerned for the needs of community members, no matter their religious affiliation.
Western Kentucky Catholic photo

Receiving Holy Orders

Father Mike Williams, right, hugs a fellow priest during the "Kiss of Peace" after being ordained a Catholic priest at Owensboro's RiverPark Center on June 1, 1997. Four priests were ordained by Bishop John McRaith in the two-hour ceremony.
Messenger-Inquirer photo by Will Chandler

Morning Prayers

Student Luke Searcy and Father Frank Roof in morning prayers at St. Sebastian in Calhoun on March 21, 1997. With the first building in 1871, St. Sebastian began as a mission church attached to a succession of nearby parishes. St. Sebastian became an independent parish in 1962.
Submitted by Diocesan Archives

GOLDEN CELEBRATIONS

A celebration of the Mass in Blessed Mother parish church in 1998 commemorating the life and death of Jesus, the 50 years of priestly ministry of Father Phil Riney, and the 50th anniversary of Blessed Mother Parish in Owensboro.
Submitted by Rev. C.P. Riney

ON HIS WAY

This 1990 picture of Father Howard Tucker on his moped was a familiar sight in Owensboro. Father Tucker, a former Benedictine monk, used it to visit the homebound and bring them the Sacraments. He was a construction company owner before entering religious life, and often used his own money to help people in need. He also made and sold concrete statues of the Blessed Mother to earn money for the poor.
Submitted by April Dickens

FRIENDS

Priest friends gather in the St. Martin rectory in Rome during a 1997 Forty Hours devotion at the parish. From left are Father Joe O'Donnell, G.H.M.S., Father Phil Riney, Father Carl Glahn, Father Joe Mills, Father Clarence Hite, Father Charlie Fischer, Father B.J. Hagman and Father Emil Schuwey, C.PP.S.
Submitted by Father Joe Mills

20TH ANNIVERSARY

Delaney Bell, 5, left, a student at St. Mary Elementary School in Paducah, and Hannah Hagan, 6, a student at St. Angela Merici School in Owensboro, make a final check on a wagon loaded with cards expressing good wishes to the Most Reverend John J. McRaith, bishop of the Diocese of Owensboro. The cards were from students throughout the diocese and were presented to McRaith near the end of a Mass at St. Stephen Cathedral on Dec. 15, 2002, celebrating his 20 years as bishop of the diocese. *Messenger-Inquirer photo by Robert Bruck*

PAPAL VISIT

Bishop John J. McRaith's fifth ad limina visit to Pope John Paul II was in December 2004. The Holy Father passed away not long after on April 2, 2005. *Submitted by Diocesan Archives*

FOND FAREWELL

The Most Rev. John J. McRaith, Bishop of the Diocese of Owensboro, center, with the Diocesan staff. On January 6, 2009, Bishop John J. McRaith announced to the Diocesan staff in the Catholic Pastoral Center that he was resigning as the third Bishop of Owensboro due to health reasons. On Jan. 7, 2009, Reverend Michael Clark, then Judicial Vicar, became the interim Diocesan Administrator until a new bishop was ordained for the diocese. *Submitted by Diocesan Archives*

SHOW OF RESPECT

Joe Danzer, right, kisses Rev. William Francis Medley's hand on Dec. 15, 2009, after Medley was announced as the next bishop of the Diocese of Owensboro at Brescia University. Danzer said the kiss is, "a sign of respect for our new bishop."
Messenger-Inquirer photo by Jenny Sevcik

VESPERS

The Rev. William Francis Medley, Bishop-elect of Owensboro, center, signs a profession of faith as the Most Rev. John J. McRaith, Bishop Emeritus of Owensboro, right, and Sister Jospeh Angela Boone, O.S.U., the Chancellor of the Diocese of Owensboro, left, witness on Tuesday, Feb. 9, 2010, during a Vespers service at St. Stephen Cathedral. Bishop-elect Medley's ordination ceremony was held at 2 p.m. the next day at the Sportscenter in Owensboro.
Messenger-Inquirer photo by Gary Emord-Netzley

RING AND MITER

The ecclesiastical ring and miter were laid out before the ordination of Bishop William Francis Medley on Feb. 10, 2010. The miter is a tall folding cap, consisting of two similar parts rising to a peak and sewn together at the sides. Two short lappets always hang down from the back. In the Catholic Church, the right to wear the miter is confined by Canon Law to bishops and to abbots, as it appears in the ceremony of consecration of a bishop and blessing of an abbot. The proper color of a miter is always white, although in liturgical usage white also includes vestments made from gold and silver fabrics. The embroidered bands and other ornaments which adorn a miter and the lappets may be of other colors and often are. *Messenger-Inquirer photo by Gary Emord-Netzley*

BISHOP EMERITUS

Vickie Osborne hugs the Most Rev. John McRaith on Feb. 10, 2010, as McRaith prepares to enter the main floor of the Owensboro Sportscenter with Archbishop Joseph E. Kurtz, center, and Seminarian Brandon Williams during the ordination service of his successor, the Most Rev. William Francis Medley. Bishop McRaith announced his retirement in 2009. *Messenger-Inquirer photo by Jenny Sevcik*

CROSIER

The crosier given to the Most Rev. William Francis Medley at his ordination on Feb. 10, 2010, was a gift from the priests of the Diocese of Owensboro. The crosier is shaped like a shepherd's crook. A bishop bears this staff as shepherd of the flock of God. A bishop usually holds his crosier with his left hand, leaving his right hand free to bestow blessings. The crosier is conferred upon a bishop during his ordination to the episcopacy. *Messenger-Inquirer photo by Gary Emord-Netzley*

WITNESSING HISTORY

Patti Gutiérrez, left, holds her 5-month-old son Gabriel Gutiérrez during the ordination service of the Most Rev. William Francis Medley on Feb. 10, 2010, at the Owensboro Sportscenter. Medley is the fourth bishop of the Diocese of Owensboro.
Messenger-Inquirer photo by Jenny Sevcik

PROCESSION

The Most Rev. William Francis Medley, center, sings along with other priests and bishops, Knights of Columbus and the people of the Diocese of Owensboro, as he processes into the Sportscenter to begin his ordination and installation service on Feb. 10, 2010.
Messenger-Inquirer photo by Gary Emord-Netzley

CONSECRATION
Newly-ordained Bishop William Francis Medley uses a thurible – a metal censer suspended from chains containing burning incense – to incense the bread and wine during Mass on Feb. 10, 2010. *Messenger-Inquirer photo by Gary Emord-Netzley*

PROSTRATE
The Most Rev. William Francis Medley prostrates himself during his ordination as the fourth bishop of the Diocese of Owensboro on Feb. 10, 2010. *Messenger-Inquirer photo by Jenny Sevcik*

Marriage
Sacred Covenant Between Man and Woman

The Catholic church teaches that marriage is a way to respond to God's call to holiness and be a sign of Christ's love in the world. Marriage unites a man and woman in faithful and mutual love.

Marriage is the only Catholic sacrament which is not bestowed by an ordained priest. A priest or deacon will witness as the man and woman bestow the sacrament on each other. The ability to confer a sacramental marriage on each other requires that the two participants be one man and one woman, that they be baptized, that they be free to marry, that they willingly and knowingly enter into a valid marriage contract, and that they validly execute the performance of the contract.

The Catholic church provides preparation leading up to the marriage date to help the couple form their consent. The Church offers many resources for couples at any point in their marriage preparation.

"For this reason a man shall leave (his) father and (his) mother and be joined to his wife, and the two shall become one flesh." This is a great mystery, but I speak in reference to Christ and the church.

Ephesians 5:31-32

Lord Jesus, on this happy day we thank you for the joy of [Name] and [Name]. Through all the years of their life you have watched over them to bring them together in holy Christian marriage. Now Lord, bless them, for they are united in love of you and of each other. Redeemed by your Precious Blood and strengthened by your grace, may they live in kindness and fidelity, in unfailing trust and love so that their whole life may be pleasing to you.

Mary, who with Joseph made a happy home at Nazareth for Jesus, take these dear friends into your motherly care. You who showed concern for a newly married couple at Cana, help and guide them. May their union on earth lead to that eternal union in which all the blessed will be joined together, praising the Redeeming Blood of Jesus, the Lord. Amen.

Dedication of the Newly Married Couple to the Precious Blood

Nuptial Mass

Father Lucian Paul Hayden officiates at a wedding in St. Stephen Cathedral in Owensboro in 1949. He was ordained in June of that year and served as assistant pastor at St. Stephen until 1958. *Submitted by Margaret Montgomery*

I Do

Father Joe O'Donnell officiates at a wedding on May 13, 1989 at St. John the Baptist Church in Fordsville. Father O'Donnell was a Glenmary Home Missioner for 63 years before his death in 2009. *Submitted by Margaret Montgomery*

GOLDEN ANNIVERSARY

John and Gail Kelly, at left, members of St. Mary Parish since 1959, celebrated their 50th wedding anniversary with their Church family on Sept. 9, 2008 in the parish hall. Mrs. Kelly served as chairperson of the parish finance committee during the years of planning and building the large expansion of facilities in Franklin.The Kellys are the proud parents of five sons. Parishioners at right are Tracee and Mike Cremeens and Karen Trouten. *Submitted by St. Mary Parish Archive*

Anointing of the Sick
For Bodily Healing and Forgiveness of Sins

The Sacrament of Anointing of the Sick offers grace for someone with any severity of illness or injury. Through the sacrament, a gift of the Holy Spirit is given to strengthen faith and banish discouragement throughout recovery. For anyone near death, the sacrament – sometimes referred to as Last Rites – also includes Reconciliation and Communion if they are able.

Anointing of the Sick is a sacrament which can be offered by any priest – and, in fact, priests may carry the Holy Chrism with them at any time, should a need arise. The sacrament can be repeated for each illness or a significant worsening of condition.

The actual anointing of the sick person is done on the forehead, with the prayer "Through this holy anointing may the Lord in his love and mercy help you with the grace of the Holy Spirit," and on the hands, with the prayer "May the Lord who frees you from sin save you and raise you up." To each prayer the sick person, if able, responds: "Amen."

> Is anyone among you sick? He should summon the presbyters of the church, and they should pray over him and anoint (him) with oil in the name of the Lord, and the prayer of faith will save the sick person, and the Lord will raise him up. If he has committed any sins, he will be forgiven.
> *James 5:14-15*

Dear Jesus, Divine Physician and Healer of the sick, we turn to you in this time of illness. O dearest Comforter of the troubled, alleviate our worry and sorrow with your gentle love, and grant us the grace and strength to accept this burden. Dear God, we place our worries in your hands. We place our sick under your care and humbly ask that you restore your servant to health again. Above all, grant us the grace to acknowledge your will and know that whatever you do, you do for the love of us. Amen.
Prayer for the Sick

SHIELDED

Catholics frequently carry on their person or in their car a small shield or other emblem saying that they are a Catholic, and in the event of an accident, to call a priest who can administer the "last rites", or the sacraments of Anointing of the Sick, Reconciliation and/or Eucharist, depending on the extent of their injuries. *Submitted by Diocesan Archives*

GAINING SPIRITUAL STRENGTH

Father Gregory Trawick administers the Anointing of the Sick to Brennan Mattingly at St. Alphonsus Church in St. Joseph on March 25, 2000. Brennan was diagnosed with leukemia in December 1999 at age 4. At the time of publication in 2010, Brennan was in remission.
Submitted by Bob and Ann Mattingly

FINAL MASS

The funeral Mass of Bishop Francis R. Cotton was held at St. Stephen Cathedral in Owensboro on Sept. 28, 1960.
Submitted by Diocesan Archives

Gary Netzley, Messenger-Inquirer

Eight bishops and Archbishop Thomas Kelly of Louisville celebrate a funeral Mass for retired Bishop Henry J. Soenneker at St. Stephen Cathe- dral Monday. Some 700 people attended services for Soenneker.

Flock bids farewell to Soenneker

By Karen Owen
Messenger-Inquirer

The Most Rev. Henry J. Soennek- er's spiritual flock gathered Mon- day to bid farewell to a shepherd described as generous with others but frugal with himself.

The retired bishop, who died Thursday at the age of 80, used to cook his own chicken soup and con- tinued driving cars when they had 90,000 miles on them. But he left behind a diocese that was financial- ly sound, Soenneker's successor said at the funeral.

"We could not be doing some things we're doing if not for his good stewardship," the Most Rev. John J. McRaith told the approxi- mately 700 people at St. Stephen Ca- thedral.

The crowd filled the church, and at times, people in the back stood on tiptoe to get a better look as Archbishop Thomas Kelly of Louis- ville; eight bishops or retired bish- ops, including McRaith, and about 90 diocesan priests celebrated Mass.

The spicy smell of incense wafted

through the interior at times, and a diocesan choir sang hymns in Latin as well as English.

A few women in the audience wore the lace veils that used to be used for the required head cover- ings at Mass. Some wore nursing uniforms, as if they were on their way to or from work.

Completing the cycle from birth to death to anticipated resur- rection, Soenneker's closed casket was blessed with holy water, just as he had been baptized as a baby, and it was covered with a white cloth,

just as he had been dressed in a white garment after his baptism.

The Roman Catholic Diocese of Owensboro owes much to Soennek- er, McRaith told the group.

Soenneker was an effective lead- er during a time of change for the church and society, through the civ- il rights movement, the Vietnam War and the changes initiated by the Second Vatican Council, McR- aith said.

Soenneker served as bishop of the

See **BISHOP/BACK PAGE**

FAREWELL
Archbishop Thomas Kelly sprinkles holy water on the casket of retired Bishop Henry J. Soenneker at his Sept. 28, 1987, funeral Mass.
Messenger-Inquirer photo by Gary Emord-Netzley

HOLY OILS
Delegates from St. Joseph Parish in Leitchfield receive the holy oils from Bishop John J. McRaith at the Chrism Mass at the Sportscenter in Owensboro in 1988. *Western Kentucky Catholic photo by Mel Howard*

FATHER LAUZON
The funeral Mass of Father Peter E. Lauzon in August 1995. Father Lauzon was ordained on Jan. 6, 1979. *Submitted by Diocesan Archives*

BLESSINGS
Sister Michele Morek, congregational leader of the Ursuline Sisters of Mount Saint Joseph, sprinkles holy water over the graves of Ursuline nuns buried in the cemetery on Aug. 6, 2005, during a blessing ceremony. The blessing is part of an annual celebration marking the Ursuline's becoming an autonomous order on Aug. 5, 1911. At the time of the ceremony, Sister Michele Morek was in the second year of a six-year leadership term. *Messenger-Inquirer photo by Gary Emord-Netzley*

SANCTITY OF LIFE
Sister Alicia Coomes, O.S.U., and Sister Judith Nell Riney, O.S.U., at a vigil before the execution of Harold McQueen at Eddyville on June 30, 1997. The Catholic Church is in the vanguard of the opposition to capital punishment. Catholics believe in the sanctity of all life. *Submitted by Diocesan Archives*

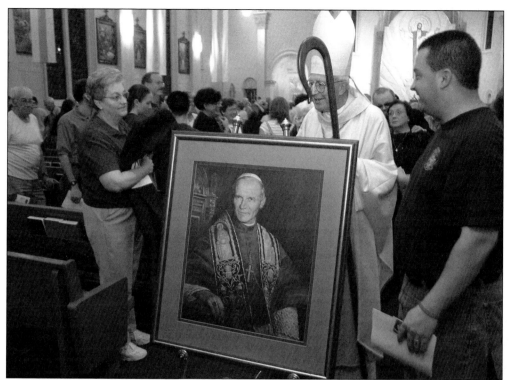

PAPAL MEMORIAL

The Most Rev. John J. McRaith, bishop of the Roman Catholic Diocese of Owensboro, center, greets parishoners at the conclusion of a memorial Mass for Pope John Paul II on April 4, 2005, at St. Stephen Cathedral. *Messenger-Inquirer photo by Gary Emord-Netzley*

DEATH PENALTY PROTEST

Sister Alicia Coomes, O.S.U., and Father Suresh Bakka, H.G.M., an associate pastor of St. Stephen Cathedral, participate in a peaceful protest against capital punishment on the steps of the federal courthouse at Frederica and West Fifth streets on Nov. 11, 2008. Sister Suzanne Sims, O.S.U., organized the protest because of the scheduled execution of Marco Allen Chapman at the Kentucky State Penitentiary in Eddyville. Chapman was sentenced to death after pleading guilty to the murders of two children in 2004. Sims said, "We think that atrocious crimes like this should be punished by life in prison without parole. Life is precious no matter who they are and what they've done. It's up to God to judge him." *Messenger-Inquirer photo by Jenny Sevcik*

Consecrated Life
Men and Women Living Close to God

Each day faithful men and women who are called to follow Jesus Christ, take public vows and commit themselves, for the love of God, to a wholly religious way of life. These vows can include chastity, poverty and obedience to a specific religious order or community.

While only men can be ordained into the Catholic priesthood, not all religious men are ordained. A lay Christian man who commits himself to Christ and a Christian community is known as a brother of that community or order. There are also communities of priests and communities including both brothers and priests.

Among religious women, "nuns" and "sisters" are distinguished by the type of vows they take and the life they lead. Nuns take solemn vows to a religious order and typically dedicate their lives to contemplation, meditation and prayer, rarely leaving their monastery, cloister or convent. Sisters usually take simple vows to their institute or congregation and they typically perform direct service work out in the world. The Code of Canon Law also allows for a Catholic woman to consecrate her virginity to God, whether or not she chooses to live as part of a religious group or on her own in the world.

> In a large household there are vessels not only of gold and silver but also of wood and clay, some for lofty and others for humble use. If anyone cleanses himself of these things, he will be a vessel for lofty use, dedicated, beneficial to the master of the house, ready for every good work. So turn from youthful desires and pursue righteousness, faith, love, and peace, along with those who call on the Lord with purity of heart.
>
> *2 Timothy 2:20-22*

Lord, through Baptism, You invite me to share the gift of my life in service to others. Be with me as I choose each day to show Your presence in our world. Give me the courage and generosity to respond to Your love, to Your call. I pray especially for those who serve You as priests, brothers, sisters and deacons. Keep them close to You. Open the minds and hearts of many other men and women to be witnesses to Your Gospel. Amen.

Prayer for Vocations

First Council

The first elected Council for the Mount St. Joseph Ursulines in 1913 included, left to right, Sister Angela Kohl, Sister Agnes O'Flynn, Mother Aloysius Willett and Sister Mercedes Wathen. Mother Aloysius had been the local Mother Superior since 1905 and Mother Augustine Bloemer had held the position before her, but Mother Aloysius was the first Canonical Elected Mother Superior after the Ursuline Sisters of Mt. St. Joseph were approved by the Holy See to become an independent and autonomous community in 1912. *Submitted by Diocesan Archives*

Sister of Charity of Nazareth

Sisters of Charity of Nazareth gather for a celebration at St. Jerome in Fancy Farm in 1925. Many of these sisters ministered in the diocesan Catholic schools. *Submitted by the Sisters of Charity of Nazareth*

Twice Sisters

These three blood sisters entered the Sisters of Charity of Nazareth together on Sept. 24, 1933. They are Sister Lucy Carrico, left, Sister Angela Maria Carrico and Sister Ann Maria Carrico. Sister Angela Maria, center, is wearing the nurse's habit while the other two are wearing the teacher's habit. At that time, most of the Sisters of Charity of Nazareth worked in either nursing or teaching. *Submitted by Ruth Ann Carrico*

Sisters of Providence

Sister Mary Laurina (Anna) Kestler, of the Sisters of Providence, in Kentucky in 1930. Sister Mary Laurina passed away on April 13, 1954, and is buried on the grounds of St. Mary of the Woods College in Indiana. *Submitted by Diocesan Archives*

Surveying for Mercy Hospital

The building project for Our Lady of Mercy Hospital in Owensboro, sponsored by the Sisters of Mercy, began with surveying the land in 1944. The hospital's name was changed to Mercy Hospital in 1984. When the facililty merged with another local hospital in 1995, the name became Owensboro Mercy Health System and then Owensboro Medical Health System. The original facility was replaced by the HealthPark, a facility focused on improving the community's health through preventative care, in 1997. The five components of the new HealthPark included a physical development and rehabilitation center, outpatient diagnostic services, a health resource center, physician offices and a chapel. *Submitted by Diocesan Archives*

BEGINNINGS

The five Passionist Sisters to come to Owensboro to establish their new convent in 1946 were Mother Mary Cecilia, Sister Mary Agnes, Sister Jeanne Marie, Sister Mary Bernadette and Sister Frances Marie. The convent began in a home on Benita Avenue and later moved to a new facility on Crisp Road near Whitesville.
Submitted by Diocesan Archives

CONTEMPLATION

The five foundresses of St. Joseph Monastery for the Discalced Nuns of the Most Holy Cross and Passion of Our Lord Jesus Christ – commonly referred to as the Passionist Nuns – at the time of their relocation from Scranton, Penn., to Owensboro in 1946. Mother Mary Agnes Roche is seated in front. St. Joseph Monastery was established at the former Monarch home at 1420 Benita Avenue in Owensboro. The home was later razed to make way for a new building on the site. In 1995, the group moved to a new facility on 150 acres they purchased on Crisp Road near Whitesville. The Passionists are cloistered, which means they live in seclusion and seldom leave their convent or allow the outside world to intrude on their regimen of work and prayer.
Submitted by Ruth Ann Carrico

Sisters of Charity

A family potrait taken at a reunion of the Charles R. Carrico family in the summer of 1947 at the family home in St. Lawrence Parish. Front row, left to right: Virginia Boarman Carrico, Charles R. Carrico, Elizabeth Johnson Carrico and Charles Edwin Carrico. Back row, left to right: Gerald Emmanuel Carrico and his wife Oda Mae, Sister Angela Maria Carrico, Sister Charles Elizabeth (Lucy) Carrico, Sister Ann Maria Carrico, Mary William Boteler Carrico and her husband Henry Ignatius Carrico. The children are Jeannette, Patrick and Ruth Ann Carrico. All three daughters entered the Sisters of Charity of Nazareth on Sept. 24, 1933 and tooks vows on March 25, 1935. All three are wearing the habit of teachers.
Submitted by Ruth Ann Carrico

Sisters of Loretta

Three Sisters of Loretta stand in front of Immaculate Conception School in
82 Hawesville on Feb. 3, 1948. *Submitted by Diocesan Archives*

Teacher and Friend

Sister Victoria, S.C.N., a senior class teacher at St. Frances Academy in Owensboro in 1948 is pictured dressed in the habit of her congregation, the Sisters of Charity of Nazareth, accompanied by two unidentified children.
Submitted by the Sisters of Charity of Nazareth

SPECIAL CALLING

Sister Rita Marie Boteler and Sister Rose Mary Boteler were among four young women from Knottsville to enter the Passionist community at St. Joseph Monastery in Owensboro over a four-year period. Sister Rose Mary was the first of the four and entered the community in 1947. Sister Rita Marie was the last when she entered in 1950. Their pastor was Father Robert Whelan. These women were the first from the local area to join the order which was established in Owensboro in 1946.
Submitted by Ruth Ann Carrico

A DEDICATED LIFE

Sister Mary Eileen Howard, O.S.U., in 1953 at St. Thomas More School in Paducah.
Submitted by Diocesan Archives

VESTITION DAY

The family of Sister Rita Marie Boteler and Sister Rose Marie Boteler at the Passionist Monastery in Owensboro in 1951 to celebrate Vestition Day for Sister Rita Marie. On their Vestition Day, a young woman receives her religious name and dons a habit for the first time to become a novice.
Submitted by Ruth Ann Carrico

Glenmary Sisters

Glenmary Sisters in Cincinnati, Ohio, in 1954. The Glenmary Home Mission Sisters of America, founded in 1941 in Cincinnati by Father William Howard Bishop, moved their headquarters to Owensboro and Livermore in 1991.
Submitted by Glenmary Sisters

The Faculty

Sisters of Charity of Nazareth who were on the faculty of St. Mary Academy in Paducah in 1958.
Submitted by the Sisters of Charity of Nazareth

Farewell

Father Victor Boarman presented a parting gift from Our Lady of Lourdes Parish in Owensboro to Sister Mary Elaine, S.C.N., as she was leaving the parish Catholic school for her new assignment during the 1960s.
Submitted by Our Lady of Lourdes Parish

Family of Service

Sister Mary Eva Thompson, left, with Brother Martin Mattingly and Sister Paul Joseph Mattingly in Daviess County in September 1967.
Submitted by Bob and Ann Mattingly

Blessing the Flag

The American flag is blessed at St. Maur Priory in South Union during the 1960s. St. Maur Priory, an interracial seminary, was founded by the Benedictines in 1947 with a small seminary and a rural life emphasis. St. Maur moved to Indianapolis in 1967.
Submitted by Ruth Ann Carrico

REUNION

Sisters of Charity of Nazareth who have served in parishes and schools in the Diocese of Owensboro gathered at St. Jerome Church in Fancy Farm in 1986 for a celebration.
Submitted by the Sisters of Charity of Nazareth

GLENMARY SISTER

Sister Kathleen Mulchrone, G.H.M.S., praying in 1980.
Submitted by Glenmary Sisters

ST. ANGELA CONVENT

A group stands in front of the St. Angela Convent in Benton on Aug. 22, 1984. Pictured are Sister Joseph Angela Boone, O.S.U., Sister Jane Irvin Hancock, O.S.U., Sister Aloise Boone, O.S.U., and Sister Therese Margaret Mattingly with Jack Blandford and Joe Riney.
Submitted by Diocesan Archives

IN THE STANDS
Sister Marie Goretti Browning serves drinks in the stands at the annual picnic at Mt. St. Joseph in 1987.
Submitted by Diocesan Archives

BLESSING THE MOTHERHOUSE
Bishop John J. McRaith and Sister Mary Joseph Wade, G.H.M.S., during a blessing of the new central office of the Glenmary Sisters at 405 West Parrish Avenue in Owensboro in 1991. The sisters relocated their motherhouse to Owensboro from from Cincinnati, Ohio.
Submitted by Glenmary Sisters

LUNCH TIME
Sister Mary Agnes of the Sisters of the Lamb of God prepares meal trays for residents at the Bishop Soenneker Home, a senior care facility in Knottsville, on March 14, 1995.
Messenger-Inquirer photo by Gary Emord-Netzley

GATHERING OF KNIGHTS
Bishop John J. McRaith prays with a Council of the Knights of Columbus in the Diocese of Owensboro. *Western Kentucky Catholic photo*

SISTER MARY AGNES
Sister Mary Agnes, C.P., Superior of the Discalced Nuns of the Most Holy Cross and Passion of Our Lord Jesus Christ, on Nov. 26, 1995 at the order's new monastery on Crisp Road near Whitesville. The order is more commonly known as the Passionist Nuns. They moved to their new monastery from their former location on Benita Avenue in Owensboro. *Messenger-Inquirer photo by Gary Emord-Netzley*

WORKING FOR TORTURE ABOLITION
Sister Sharon Sullivan, a member of the Ursuline order, wipes tears from her eyes on May 3, 1996, while listening to supporters of Sister Dianna Ortiz on the steps of the federal building in Owensboro. "The first time I met her we were down at English Park and she was writing JESUS in the sand," she said. "She was the most gentle person in the community." Sister Dianna, who is a Brescia graduate and an Ursuline Sister from Mount St. Joseph, taught parochial school in Owensboro and Hawesville before she went to Guatemala in 1987 to do mission work with poor Mayan children. Two years later, the 31-year-old was kidnapped from the garden of a retreat center, escaping about 24 hours later to tell a harrowing story of being gang raped, burned more than 100 times with cigarettes and lowered into a rat-infested pit of dead bodies. *Messenger-Inquirer photo by Robert Bruck*

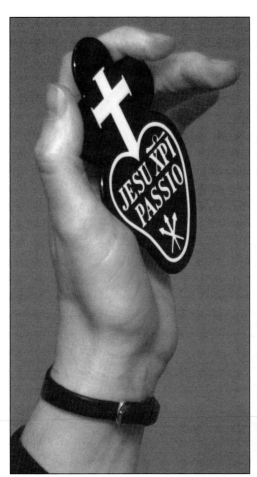

BADGE OF FAITH
Sister John Mary, C.P., explains the meaning of the Passionist badge to Brescia University students on April 9, 2001, at the Passionist monestery in Whitesville. "Jesu" is Hebrew for Jesus. "XPI" is greek for Christ. "Passio" is Latin for Passion.
Messenger-Inquirer photo by John Dunham

SISTERS OF THE DIVINE HEART OF JESUS
Sister Francis Teresa, D.C.J., administrator and local convent superior of the Carmelite Sisters of the Divine Heart of Jesus, visits with a resident at the Carmel Home in Owensboro on Aug. 21, 1997. The facility opened in 1952. Sister Francis Teresa said she "just fell in love with the older poeple," after joining the convent at age 21. "They think we are the holy ones," she said, "But they don't realize that we see holiness in them."
Messenger Inquirer photo by Cathy Clarke

QUIET CONTEMPLATION
The Passionist nuns gather for evening vespers on April 9, 2001, at their monastery on Crisp Road in Whitesville. Passionists take vows of chastity, poverty, obedience and silence.
Messenger-Inquirer photo by John Dunham

Reliving the Journey

Sister Larraine Lauter, right, looks for her fellow Ursuline Sisters as she and Sister Amelia Stenger, center, greet friends, family and media before beginning a 5-day flatboat journey to Owensboro on Aug. 14, 2004, in New Albany, Indiana. The voyage marks the 130th anniversary of the journey of the first five Ursuline sisters who came to Owensboro by flatboat in 1874. *Messenger-Inquirer photo by Gary Emord-Netzley*

Angela's Ark

Angela's Ark takes a test run on Aug. 12, 2005, on the Ohio River near the boat dock at the foot of Frederica Street in Owensboro. Ursuline Sister Amelia Stenger of Mount St. Joseph said the flatboat was used in 2004 to re-enact the original 1874 trip of five Ursuline sisters down the Ohio River from Louisville to Owensboro. "We had to take it for a test drive before our two hour tour later this afternoon," Sister Amelia said. "It floats like a dream." For the next few mornings, Ursuline sisters were given the chance to ride the flatboat. *Messenger-Inquirer photo by John Dunham*

LITURGY OF THE HOURS
Passionist nuns pray the Liturgy of the Hours at St. Joseph Monastery and Retreat House at Whitesville in 2006. Monks and nuns have been praying the Divine Office, as it is also known, for centuries. Lay people and even Protestants have been showing interest in the devotional practice in recent years.
Sumitted by St. Joseph Monastery and Retreat House

FINAL PROFESSION
Sister Sharon Miller, G.H.M.S., left, watches as Darlene Presley, G.H.M.S., makes her final profession of vows as a Glenmary Sister in Owensboro on June 7, 2008. Bishop John J. McRaith, right, officiated at the service with Father John Vaughn's assistance. Sister Sharon is the community president for the Glenmary Home Mission Sisters.
Submitted by Glenmary Sisters

Nature Lesson

Sister Eula Johnson, S.C.N., second from right, walks with, from left, Luis Cruz, 13, Emperatriz González, 47, Esmeralda Cruz, 15, and Mayra Cruz, 17, along Littlewood Drive in Owensboro, giving them a lesson on the names of the beautiful plants and trees that line the street. "I taught these children English as a second language," Sister Eula Johnson said. The family, which is from Acapulco, Mexico, moved to Owensboro in 2009. *Messenger-Inquirer photo by Gary Emord-Netzley*

COMMUNITY DAYS

Glenmary Home Mission Sisters and Postulants in 2010 during their Community Days in Owensboro. The Glenmary Sisters Community comes together twice a year to reflect, renew, recommit and relax. The week begins with two days of prayer and reflection followed by community meetings, a business day and, in the Fall, a Mission Sending ceremony. Front row, left to right: Postulant Justine Presley, Sister Ellen Frances Lenihan, Sister Kathleen Mulchrone, Sister Mary Ellen Barrette and Sister Sharon Miller, community president. Back row, left to right: Sister Catherine Schoenborn, Sister Rosemary Esterkamp, Sister Aida Badillo, Sister Bernadette Hengstebeck, Sister Darlene Presley and Postulant Pam Hageman.
Submitted by Glenmary Sisters

HAPPY BIRTHDAY

Bishop John McRaith, left, poses with Sister Fran Wilhelm, O.S.U., during her 80th birthday celebration at the SS. Joseph & Paul Parish Hall in Owensboro in January 2009. Sister Fran founded Centro Latino, which administers aid to Hispanics in the Owensboro area. Also a musician, Sister Fran frequently provides musical accompaniment for the Spanish Masses at the parish.
Submitted by April Dickens

Catholic Education
Pairing faith with educaton

In the United States, Catholics and non-Catholics take advantage of Catholic educational programs at all levels – elementary and secondary schools, religious education programs, colleges, universities and seminaries. Catholic schools are known for traditionally high academic standards and high graduation rates, all supported by the reinforcement of strong moral values.

The Mission of the Catholic Schools of the Diocese of Owensboro is to share in the Church's mission, to proclaim the message of Jesus Christ as lived out in the Catholic Church which creates a worshiping community of believers whose service is a witness of their Christian love.

With a special emphasis on faith formation, high academic standards and a safe school environment, Catholic schools offer an alternative for families seeking a Christian education. They uphold a standard of order and discipline to teach students responsibility, accountability and respect for themselves and others. Additionally, Catholic schools prepare each student for adult life through the teachings of Jesus Christ and His Church.

> **Your hands made me and fashioned me; give me insight to learn your commands.**
> *Psalms 119:73*

For those Catholic children who choose to attend public schools or do not have access to a Catholic school, parishes offer classes in religious education. These classes are often held on Sunday or in the evening one night during the week. During these classes, children are taught the doctrine of the faith, formed in the liturgy, develop moral character, learn to pray, grow in understanding of living in community and begin to develop a missionary spirit.

God, our Father and Creator, be with us in our school. Help us to treasure Your gift of life and treat one another with care. Let us always remember that we are all created in Your image. Come, Lord Jesus, and be with us in our school. Guide our teachers, guide our parents, and lead our students to recognize You in all people. Come, Holy Spirit, and be with us in our school. Give us a vision for the future, and the determination for shaping a faith-filled future. Amen.

A Prayer for Schools

School Boys

The boys from the Chapel School held in the church building in St. Paul parish in Leitchfield in 1837 a full 100 years before the Diocese of Owensboro was formed. When Father Charles Nerincx built the church in 1810, it was known as St. James parish. The first official school building for the parish was not constructed until 1908 under the leadership of Father Anthony Helling. Increased attendance required that the school be expanded from one room to two in 1912. *Submitted by Deanna Kipper*

Academy for Girls

Mt. St. Joseph Academy students on the front steps of their school in the late 1800s or early 1900s. In 1874, Father Paul Joseph Volk asked the Ursulines to establish St. Joseph Academy for girls at Maple Mount. *Submitted by Diocesan Archives*

ST. VINCENT ACADEMY

Sisters of Charity of Nazareth staffed the St. Vincent Academy in Union County, founded in 1820, located near Sacred Heart church. In this undated photo of St. Vincent Academy students, the young women are dressed in the school uniform of the day, complete with mortar board headwear. *Submitted by the Sisters of Charity of Nazareth*

FIRST SCHOOL

Chickens peck the ground and children peek from the doorway in this undated photo of St. Lawrence School in Philpot. The first pastor of St. Lawrence, Father John Wathen, established the school in about 1833. His may have been the first parochial school in Daviess County. *Submitted by Millie Carrico*

St. Lawrence School

St. Frances Academy Basketball

The St. Frances Academy basketball team from 1928-1929. Standing, from left: Robert "Pike" Connor, Joe Millay, Joe Castlen, Father Nieters Cyril Oberst and Eugene Greenwell. Seated, from left: Tom Libs, Pete Grinas, Cecil Oberst, Les Whalen and Tom Monarch. Robert Connor and Tom Libs both later became priests. Father Connor taught and coached at St. Frances Academy. *Submitted by Joe Castlen*

St. Joseph Graduates

The 1939 8th grade graduating class of St. Joseph School, Bowling Green. Front row, left to right: Tommy Murphy, Spencer Monahan, H.G. Cecil, Dennis Nunan, Henry Dunkins. Back row, left to right: Joan Dienes, Patty Nusz, Juanita Johnson, Pat Gray, Paula Donnelly, Frances O'Shea. *Submitted by Bonnie Gibson*

97

FIRST CLASS
The first graduating class of Blessed Sacrament Chapel school for black Catholics in Owensboro in 1945, with Father Robert Connor. *Submitted by Veronica Wilhite*

VALEDICTORIAN

Mary William Boteler, at right, was ranked first in her 1942 graduation class at St. William in Knottsville. She received the highest award in the class for academics.
Submitted by Ruth Ann Carrico

Dorothy Jean Franey

Rev. William B. Jarboe
Pastor

Geraldine Marie Howard

ST. MARY'S SCHOOL
SENIOR CLASS
1947
Whitesville, Ky.

Elizabeth Eileen Barrett

Geneva Rosa Boyke

Mary Christine Edge

Walter Douglas Howard

Jay Shelton Aud

Inez Marie Hinton

Margaret Ann Coomes

Carl Franklin Mills

Amelia Winifred Howard

Submitted by Hazel Aud

St. Frances Academy
Owensboro's St. Frances Academy Class of 1948.
Submitted by Rita Thomas

Catholic Press Month
St. Frances Academy school newspaper students from the journalism class of 1948 celebrating Catholic Press Month in February.
Submitted by Rita Thomas

Graduation Day

Students pose for a photo at their 8th grade graduation from St. Elizabeth in Curdsville in 1951. Front row, left to right: Martin McCarty, Dennis McCarthy, Bob McCarthy, Gene Schadler, Bill Calhoun, Barbara Calhoun, Paul Payne, Sylvester Higdon and Tom Murphy. Back, left to right: Jerome McCarty, Father Henry Willett, Jo Ann Payne, Margie Byrne, Patty Mahoney, Jeanetta Payne, Joan Payne, Rita McCarthy, Edwina Fenwick, Ruth Ann Higdon, Eleanor Clements, Sister Clarencia and Peggy Murphy. St. Elizabeth School was opened in September 1911. *Submitted by Peggy McCarthy*

Proud Graduates

The 8th grade class gathered for a portrait after graduation at St. Alphonsus School near Owensboro in 1952. Back row, left to right: Sister Rose Catherine, Richard Hodskins, Raymond Thomas, Larry Robinson, Robert Mattingly, James Clouse, Kenny Stallings, James Higdon, Damien Alvey, Charles Fulkerson, William Payne, Edward Clouse, Richard Blandford and Philip O'Bryan. Front row, left to right: Terry Blandford, Larry Blandford, Faye Murphy, Shelby Hayden, Bernice Dant, Barbara Vowels, Madge Riney, Martha Johnson, Bonnie Payne, Junior Rummage, James Dockemeyer and Father Joseph McAleer. *Submitted by Bob and Ann Mattingly*

St. William Graduates

Members of the St. William High School Class of 1942 in their caps and gowns. Mary William Boteler is seated at left. St. William Parish is located in Knottsville. *Submitted by Ruth Ann Carrico*

101

STURDY CROSS

Chickens wander in the school yard at St. Mary of the Woods School in Whitesville in the early 1950s. Scaffolding surrounds the top of the bell tower above the convent which housed the school's faculty, the Sisters of Charity of Nazareth. Some parishioners remember when the late Ivo Howard, who helped build the school, climbed to the top of the bell tower to stand on the arms of the cross to show Pastor Msgr. Hugh O'Sullivan that the cross was bolted well enough to withstand high winds. *Submitted by Christine Edge Mulligan*

SCHOOL MASS

St. Joseph School Mass led by Father Lucian Paul Hayden in Central City in December 1959. Father Hayden was the pastor of St. Joseph and the Mission of St. Charles in Livermore from 1958 to 1966. *Submitted by Margaret Montgomery*

GOLDEN JUBILEE

The 5th grade class at St. Mary of the Woods School in Whitesville during the 1951-1952 school year. According to records of the Diocese of Owensboro, 320 pupils were enrolled in the school for the 1951-1952 school year. The pastor was Father Martin Nahstoll, the assistant pastor was Father Walter A. Hancock and the school principal was Sister Mary Rita, SCN. Although the first school in the parish was established in 1879, the 1951-1952 school year marked the 50th year of continuous teaching by the Sisters of Charity of Nazareth and was celebrated as a Golden Jubilee. *Submitted by the Arnold Howard Family*

FIRST DAY

It is the first day of school in the new St. Pius X in Calvert City in 1954, a mission church which was part of the St. Francis de Sales parish based in Paducah. The first Mass offered in the makeshift Catholic Church in the Legion Hall in Calvert City had been on Ash Wednesday, February 22, 1953, at 8 a.m. by Father Albert Thompson. On September 5, 1954, the Sunday before Labor Day, Bishop Francis Cotton officially dedicated the new Church. And on September 8, 1954, the two-room Catholic School opened with 21 students in grades 1 to 8. Sister Benira Tankersley, of the Sisters of Charity of Nazareth, was the first instructor and she traveled over 9,000 miles that first year to and from Paducah. In 1962, St. Pius X achieved official status as a parish. The students that first year in the St. Pius X School were Glen Brewer, Carol Elam and Nancy Stock, grade 1; Chris Zurschmeide, Anita Herring, Stephanie Wilkes, Janice Janiak and Jimmy Gootee, grade 2; Danny Brewer, Frank Tomsic, Jr., Sandra Wild and Gelbert Wild, grade 3; Janet Heise, grade 4; Janet Ziblut and Diane Heise, grade 5; Carolyn Stopher, Gloria Janiak and William Girth, grade 6; Karen Heise, grade 7; Judy Montag and Loretta Cissell, grade 8. *Submitted by Diocesan Archives from the scrapbook of the Frank and Florence Tomsic Family*

YOUTHFUL POWER

Father George Boehmicke, left, an unidentified Archbishop and Bishop Francis R. Cotton meet with Catholic Student Mission Crusade (CSMC) President Fischer at their conference in Owensboro in May 1956. The CSMC movement was founded by Father Jolly Paschal Hayden of Kentucky in 1918 and on July 20, 1935, CSMC was elevated to the dignity of a Pontifical Society by Decree of the Sacred Congregation of the Propagation of Faith. When the Diocese of Owensboro was formed in 1937, representatives of CSMC met with Bishop Cotton to tell him of their goal to have a Catholic church in every county in the diocese. Parish youth from around the diocese raised funds for the project and their goal was achieved. *Submitted by Diocesan Archives*

MISSION CRUSADE

A Catholic Students Mission Crusade (CSMC) rally at the Sportscenter in Owensboro in the late 1950s. This celebration of the history of Catholics in Kentucky was directed by Father George Boehmicke. *Submitted by Ruth Ann Carrico*

CLASS OF 1955

The Class of 1955 from St. Stephen School in Owensboro. The photo was taken on Friday, June 3, 1955.
Submitted by Pam Huff and St. Stephen Cathedral

HIGH TECH

The latest technology of the day in 1957 at Owensboro Catholic High School included typewriters for the business class. *Submitted by Marilyn Pace*

CLASS TRIP

On May 14, 1957, students from Mount St. Joseph Academy took their class trip to Mammoth Cave National Park.
Submitted by Bob and Ann Mattingly

CLASS OF 1958

The 1958 graduates of St. Stephen School in Owensboro gathered for a portrait on May 22, 1958.
Maglinger Portraits photo submitted by Pam Huff and St. Stephen Cathedral

CLASS OF 1959
The 1959 graduates of St. Stephen School in
Owensboro on May 25, 1959.
Submitted by Pam Huff and St. Stephen Cathedral

IMPORTANT LESSON
Sister Paul Joseph Mattingly, O.S.U., teaching
during the 1960s. This photo may have been
taken at St. Romuald's School in Hardinsburg,
where she taught for several years.
Submitted by Bob and Ann Mattingly

Class of 1961

The St. Stephen School graduating class of 1961 displays their diplomas for a portrait. *Arrow Studio photo submitted by Pam Huff and St. Stephen Cathedral*

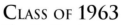

Class of 1962

St. Stephen Class of 1962 stands in front of the Cathedral altar in Owensboro. *Submitted by Pam Huff and St. Stephen Cathedral*

Class of 1963

The St. Stephen graduating class of 1963 in front of the altar in the Cathedral on May 28, 1963. This is one of the few photographs available showing the former altar windows in such detail. *Graphic Art Studio photo by Robert D. Chambers submitted by Pam Huff and St. Stephen Cathedral*

Marian Medal

The 1965 St. Stephen Girl Scout Troop #224 was the first in Owensboro to have members receive the Marian Award. Front, left to right: Donna Fulkerson, Janie Monarch, Kathy Haase and Debby Haynes. Back, left to right: Michele Denko, Martha Monarch, Marty Kerrick and Tina Bresler. The Marian Medal program is written for young Catholics, grades 7 to 10, to enable them to proclaim the greatness of the Lord. This is accomplished by actively involving the participants in an understanding of Mary as a model of openness and spirituality—a woman of the church. Through various projects, discussions, and liturgical celebrations over a period of months, the participants are provided with a unique opportunity to develop new insights into their personalities, friends, parents, and the world around them.
Submitted by Pam Huff and St. Stephen Cathedral

On a Mission

A portion of the crowd at the Catholic Student Mission Crusade (CSMC) Rally at the Owensboro Sportscenter in spring 1965. The CSMC program was founded by a Kentucky priest, Father Lucian Hayden, in 1918. The powerful youth program ended sometime during the 1960s.
Submitted by Diocesan Archives

Class of 1960

The 1960 8th grade graduation class of Immaculate Conception Parish in Earlington posed with pastor Father William Borntrager and Sister Jeanne Mary Hardesty, O.S.U. The Catholic community at Earlington, under the title of Immaculate Conception, was established as a parish by Bishop McCloskey of Louisville on Dec. 11, 1873. The first Earlington church was dedicated on the last Sunday of August 1873. On Oct. 16, 1886, Bishop McCloskey laid the cornerstone for the new church building which was completed and blessed on May 31, 1888. *Submitted by Barbara Davis for Immaculate Conception Parish*

St. William High School

St. William High School was established in Knottsville in 1927. St. William Elementary School had been open since 1912. Students were taught first by Ursuline Sisters and later by Sisters of Charity of Nazareth. The high school was consolidated with Whitesville's St. Mary of the Woods High School in the fall of 1967 to create Trinity High School to serve students from St. Lawrence, St. William and St. Mary of the Woods Parishes. *Submitted by Millie Carrico*

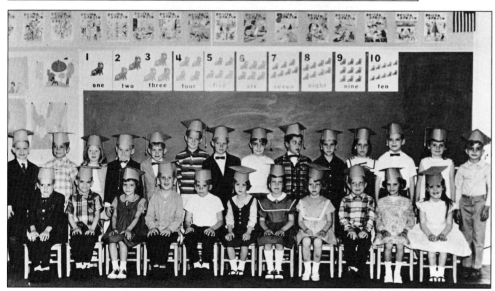

Holy Family Kindergarten

The Sisters of the Lamb of God opened the Holy Family Kindergarten in their Convent at 1516 Parrish Avenue in Owensboro in 1964. It moved to Owensboro Catholic High in 1965 and remained there until it closed in 1981. *Submitted by Judy Kapelsohn*

LAY PRINCIPAL
Joseph O'Bryan, left, in a 1979 Owensboro Catholic High School photo of the Religion Department. O'Bryan later became the school's first lay principal, serving from 1985 to 1991. Father Tony Shonis, far right, was also a member of the Religion faculty at the time.
Submitted by Harold Staples

FATHER CALHOUN
Owensboro Catholic High School's second priest principal, Father Gerald Calhoun, right, signs a yearbook for OCHS coach, teacher and assistant principal Bruce Embry in a 1974.
Submitted by Harold Staples

TEENS ENCOUNTER CHRIST
A Teens Encounter Christ (TEC) meeting at St. Francis de Sales in Paducah, circa 1976. TEC is a movement of Catholic spirituality for older adolescents and young adults. The first TEC weekend was held in 1965 and the TEC Conference was formed in 1975. The TEC Conference enjoys a liaison relationship with the United States Conference of Catholic Bishops (USCCB) through an Episcopal Moderator Emeritus, an Episcopal Moderator, and six other bishops on the TEC Committee.
Submitted by Diocesan Archives

FATHER BRADLEY

Father Ed Bradley, left, the sixth principal of Owensboro Catholic High School, is shown here in a 1983 photo talking with Bishop John J. McRaith. Since the inception of Owensboro Catholic High School in June 1951, the principals have included Sister Mary Auxilium, S.C.N., Sister Joseph Mary, S.C.N., Sister Helen Constance, S.C.N., Father Henry O'Bryan, Father Gerald Calhoun, Father Ed Bradley, Joseph O'Bryan and Harold Staples. *Submitted by Harold Staples*

ST. MARY OF THE WOODS

Father Steve Dunn, left, Bishop John J. McRaith and Father B.J. Hagman with a class from St. Mary School in St. Mary of the Woods parish in Whitesville during the 1980s. *Submitted by Diocesan Archives*

VACATION BIBLE SCHOOL

Children and teachers attend Holy Mass on the final day of the annual Vacation Bible School held at St. Mary Parish in Franklin, during June 1980. The Sanctuary is decorated with the arts and crafts created by the children, in Kindergarten through 8th grade, during the two weeks of instruction, songs, refreshments, fun and games which was a change from the more intense, 9-month CCD program. Father Del Holmes, pastor, is seated at right, the lector is unidentified, and the servers, seated at left, are Kelly King and Scott Stoll. *Submitted by St. Mary Parish Archive*

HISTORY LESSON
Father Cyprian Davis, O.S.B., speaks about the history of black Catholics during a presentation in the St. Stephen School cafeteria in November 1988. After the school closed, St. Stephen School was converted into office and meeting space for the Catholic Pastoral Center.
Western Kentucky Catholic photo

GROUNDBREAKING
Sister Amelia Stenger, O.S.U., superintendent of the Diocese of Owensboro Catholic Schools, breaks ground for St. Mary Elementary School in Paducah in March 1991. Sister Amelia, a member of the Ursuline Order, left her position at the end of the 1990-1991 school year after successfully leading the system through a consolidation period to ensure financial stability. She had been superintendent since 1985. She went on to serve as superintendent of schools for the Archdiocese of Louisville for six years, until returning to Mt. St. Joseph as director of the Retreat and Education Center in 1997. *Submitted by Diocesan Archives*

FACULTY APPRECIATION

Local men cook for a faculty dinner at Owensboro Catholic High School in May 1993. The cooks are, left to right, Dick Flaherty, Jimmy Rogers and Tom Castlen. An unknown man is watching the action. *Photo by Mel Howard*

YOUTH CRUISE

A youth ministry boat cruise aboard the Executive Queen leaves the Executive Inn Rivermont dock in Owensboro in 1993.
Photo by Mel Howard

CALLED TO TEACH

Mae Alvey, a teacher at Holy Name of Jesus School in Henderson, in her 3rd grade classroom in 1994.
Western Kentucky Catholic photo by Mel Howard

RAINBOW MASS

The Rainbow Mass for Catholic school students is held every other year at the Owensboro Sportscenter. The Sept. 23, 1994, Mass was significant because it marked the first time female altar servers were used in a diocesan Mass.
Submitted by Diocesan Archives

IN SESSION

A class is in session at St. Mary Middle School in Paducah on Aug. 17, 1994.
Photo by Mel Howard

HISTORICAL RECORD

The editors of "The Roman Catholic Diocese of Owensboro, Kentucky" are hard at work in March of 1995 at the Catholic Pastoral Center in Owensboro. Left to right: Brother Leo Willett, Sister Joseph Angela Boone, O.S.U., Sister Rose Jean Powers, O.S.U., Sister Mary Irene Cecil, O.S.U., and Mel Howard, editor of the Western Kentucky Catholic. Their 368-page volume contains a detailed history of every church and parish in the diocese. *Submitted by Diocesan Archives*

RELAXING

Students at St. Mary Middle School in Paducah relax outside after the first day of school on Aug. 17, 1994.
Photo by Mel Howard

LAY LEADERS

Father Larry McBride from the diocesan Office of Worship leads a lay presiders workshop at Our Lady of Lourdes Parish Hall on Sept. 4, 1997. *Submitted by Diocesan Archives*

EDUCATION WING

Before a 1999 expansion of facilities, catechists of St. Mary Parish in Franklin held classes in any space they could find. Here, Paul and Kathy Abell, standing, teach students in the dining room of the Rectory during CCD class in 1997. During the expansion, the old church building was transformed into six spacious classrooms and, for the first time, teachers, students and parents were proud to have an "Education Wing." Students, left to right: Chelsea Ellis, Caitlyn Abell, Paul Marsteller and Calla Hughes. *Submitted by St. Mary Parish Archive*

GRADUATE DEGREE

Bishop McRaith congratulates graduates of the Master of Science and Management program at Brescia College in Owensboro on May 10, 1997. Even though it had been operating for a few years with Level III status, Brescia officially received the "university" designation and became Brescia University in 1998. The college was the first in the city when it was founded in 1950 by the Ursuline Sisters of Mt. St. Joseph at Maple Mount. The school was under the leadership of President Sister Vivian Bowles, O.S.U., when it became Owensboro's first university. *Submitted by Diocesan Archives*

CATHOLIC SCHOOLS WEEK

A special music activity at St. Joseph School in Bowling Green during Catholic Schools Week on Jan. 29, 1997. This awareness week is sponsored by the National Catholic Education Association to highlight benefits of a Catholic education. Because of their traditionally high academic standards and high graduation rates, all supported by strong moral values, Catholic schools and their graduates make a definite, positive contribution to American society. Catholic schools give a high level of service to local communities because of the many service projects students undertake. "Giving back to the community" and "helping others" are values instilled in every Catholic school student. *Submitted by Diocesan Archives*

FATHER O'BRYAN

Father Henry O'Bryan relaxes in the Owensboro Catholic High School office just before a dedication ceremony of a new computer lab for the school in October 2002. The lab was donated by Jim Hines, owner of Premium Allied Tool. Father O'Bryan was the school's first priest principal and lived in an apartment with a chapel at the back of the school, which later served as the principal and counselors' offices. *Submitted by Harold Staples*

COURTYARD MASS

Father Brad Whistle, sacramental minister for Owensboro Catholic High School, is shown here at a weekly school Mass in 2008 in the school courtyard. *Submitted by Harold Staples*

PILGRIMS

High School students from St. Mary Parish in Franklin made a pilgrimage to the Diocesan Shrine, "Mary, Mother of the Church and Model of All Christians," on May 17, 2008. A history of the Shrine and an explanation of each of the thirteen stained-glass windows were presented by Father Ben Luther, standing at center, director of the Diocesan Marian Shrine Committee. Students prayed the Rosary, Litany of the Blessed Virgin Mary and The Magnificat. The prayer service closed with singing "Hail, Holy Queen Enthroned Above." Prominent in the background is part of the main window in the Shrine depicting "The Miracle of the Sun at Fatima" in 1917. Left to right: Robert Clark, Kate Doyle, Lucas Farley, Amanda Mohr, parent Mary Beth Farley, Father Luther, Kali Duncan, teacher Mark Pais and Matthew Clark. *Submitted by St. Mary Parish Archive*

GOD IS MIGHTY

Sister Frances Miriam Spalding, an Ursuline Sister of Mount St. Joseph, sings "The God of Israel is Mighty" on March 11, 2006, during the 19th annual Catholic Charismatic Conference at Mount St. Joseph in Maple Mount. *Messenger-Inquirer photo by John Dunham*

ALL-SCHOOL MASS

After an all-school Mass on Wednesday, March 31, 2010, at SS. Peter & Paul Church in Hopkinsville, Bishop William Medley posed for a photo with the altar servers. Pictured from left to right are: Seminarian Julio Barrera, Father Anthoni Ottagan, H.G.N., Joseph Whitfill, Marlee Thomas, Bishop William Medley, Paige Ramos, Alex Hale, Joshua Intessimone, Father John Thomas and Father Carmelo Jimenez. *Photo by Dawn C. Ligibel*

INAUGURATION

Father Larry Hostetter watches the faculty processional while standing next to Bishop John J. McRaith on Oct. 27, 2007, during Hostetter's presidential inaugural ceremony at Brescia University's quad area. Hostetter is the first non-Ursuline to hold the position as Brescia's president. *Messenger-Inquirer photo by John Dunham*

BREAKING GROUND

The groundbreaking ceremony for the new Holy Spirit Parkside Church in Bowling Green took place on Sept. 10, 2008. Wearing white construction hats are Father Jerry Riney, left, Bishop John J. McRaith, center, and Diocesan Chancellor Sister Joseph Angela Boone, O.S.U., right. *Submitted by Diocesan Archives*

MARY CARRICO MEMORIAL SCHOOL

A benefit picnic for Mary Carrico Memorial School was held on the grounds of St. Lawrence Church in 2009. Mary Carrico Memorial School was dedicated on May 5, 1963, to serve the St. William and St. Lawrence Parishes. It replaced St. William School which had been open in Knottsville since 1912. The school building was paid for by the Governor of the Virgin Islands in memory of his mother, Mary Carrico, who had been a teacher at the former St. William elementary school. Students at Mary Carrico Memorial School have been taught by Sisters of Charity of Nazareth, Ursuline Sisters and Sisters of the Lamb of God. *Submitted by Millie Carrico*

RELIGIOUS EDUCATION
Saint Pius Tenth Parish Vacation Bible School meets at the parish hall in Owensboro. *Submitted by Diocesan Archives*

PASSING ON THE FAITH
Larry Bishop was the principal of Christ The King Catholic School in Madisonville and retired in May 2010. A principal of a Roman Catholic school is a leader of daily prayer, progress in the spiritual life, and in the passing on of the faith within a Catholic school community.
Submitted by Christ The King Parish

VACATION BIBLE SCHOOL
Pastor Father Jason McClure visits the parish's Vacation Bible School in 2009 at St. Leo, Murray. The weeklong religious education program involves many people – students, catechists, youth leaders and support people. *Submitted by St. Leo Parish*

TEENS ENCOUNTER CHRIST

A Teens Encounter Christ group at St. Charles parish in Bardwell in February 2010. According to the TEC Conference website at www.tecconference.org, Teens Encounter Christ (TEC) is a movement of spirituality. It is founded and unfolds within the living traditions of the Roman Catholic Church. At its core, it is an evangelizing process which is initiated within an adult community of believers, is shared through a specially designed weekend, and is continually renewed through shared experience within a community of youth and adults. TEC's unique spiritual vision is centered in the Paschal Mystery. This core truth of our faith is not presented within the format of academic theology, but through the meshing of life with life as the Paschal Mystery is lived out in concrete human experience. TEC is a dynamic, life-giving experience in which a person is invited by the Risen Christ to open his/her heart and to share in a personal way His life, death and resurrection. Reflectively, the candidates come to see Christ's mystery relived in their own daily life cycle of struggles, joys and triumphs as they move forward on their pilgrim journey to the fullness of life with the Triune God. First row, left to right: Amy French, Christina Best, Kelsey Bennett, Crissy Stevenson, Ed Leahy, Diane Hicks. Second row, left to right: Mary Shipe, Haley Riney, Sarah Clark, Kaitlyn Jones, Alex Hayden, Krista Shupe, Kelsey Page, David Hayden, Ashley Lorenzen, Janet Wilson. Third row, left to right: Hadley Jagoe, Freddy Wilson, Sara Estes, Ashley Fowler, Angie Burgess. Fourth row, left to right: Thomas Wilson, Michelle Roberts, Brandon Barnard, Mandy Jackson, Olivia Warren, Lauren Cates, Kari Oliver, Alex King, Whitney Cossie, Lauerne Elliott, Danny Thomas. Fifth row, left to right: Lori Dant, Nate Elder, McKenzie Elter, Adam Carrico, Carli Cummins, Jessica Jones, Haylie Hobbs, Ashley Foss. Sixth row, left to right: Seth Dant, Joey Bray, Michael Ore, Daniel Hughes, Kaylee Murphy, Kelsi Woodall, Father Bob Drury, Taylor Ballard, Frank Burch. Back row, left to right: Matthew Burton, Chris Hancock, Mark Wathen, Austin Willett, Thomas Loxley, Eric Lossie, Darin Lewis, Emily Lester, John Ross, Father Mike Williams, Michael Ligibel. *Submitted by Diocesean Youth Ministry Office*

Catholic Life
Catholic Faith Touching Daily Lives

Catholic faith touches the daily lives of Catholics and non-Catholics in many ways. The ritual, ceremony and symbols of the Catholic Church serve as a constant reminder to the congregation of their relationship to God and His gifts to the world.

In the Diocese of Owensboro, individual Catholics and Catholic Parishes live their Faith by working to improve their communities and help those in need. From pregnancy counseling and adoption services to housing and feeding the homeless and working for immigration reform, Catholics are known for opening their hearts to their neighbors.

Along with making their community a better place, and often to further the funding of those efforts, Catholics enjoy a variety of fun group activities. Parish picnics are probably the best known example in the diocese. The picnics allow time for quality fellowship among parishioners while raising funds for a variety of Church and community needs.

Hail Mary, full of grace, the Lord is with Thee. Blessed art thou among women and blessed is the fruit of Thy womb, Jesus. Holy Mary, mother of God, pray for us sinners now and at the hour of our death. Amen.
Hail Mary

"When the Son of Man comes in his glory, and all the angels with him, he will sit upon his glorious throne, and all the nations will be assembled before him. And he will separate them one from another, as a shepherd separates the sheep from the goats. He will place the sheep on his right and the goats on his left. Then the king will say to those on his right, 'Come, you who are blessed by my Father. Inherit the kingdom prepared for you from the foundation of the world. For I was hungry and you gave me food, I was thirsty and you gave me drink, a stranger and you welcomed me, naked and you clothed me, ill and you cared for me, in prison and you visited me.' Then the righteous will answer him and say, 'Lord, when did we see you hungry and feed you, or thirsty and give you drink? When did we see you a stranger and welcome you, or naked and clothe you? When did we see you ill or in prison, and visit you?' And the king will say to them in reply, 'Amen, I say to you, whatever you did for one of these least brothers of mine, you did for me.'

Matthew 25:31-40

KNIGHTS OF COLUMBUS

Owensboro's Knights of Columbus Home and members on May 11, 1923. The Knights of Columbus is a men's Catholic fraternal society that strives to bring Christianity to the world, just as Christopher Columbus did. The order has been called "the strong right arm of the Church," and has been praised by popes, presidents and other world leaders, for support of the Church, programs of evangelization and Catholic education, civic involvement and aid to those in need. *Submitted by Diocesan Archives*

PARISH PICNIC

Two unknown priests picnic on the church grounds with St. Lawrence parishioners prior to 1900. The first Catholic mass in Daviess County was held at St. Lawrence by Father Charles Nerinckx of Bardstown in 1821. *Submitted by Millie Carrico*

ST. STEPHEN CHURCH

St. Stephen Church was constructed at Second and Cedar Streets in Owensboro and opened in 1842. This early 1900s photo shows the church after an 1858 expansion. The church remained at that location until a new church building was completed in 1926 at 614 Locust Street. *Submitted by Ruth Ann Carrico*

DAUGHTERS OF ISABELLA
The Owensboro Daughters of Isabella Circle #241 was started on April 15, 1923. The 136 members were photographed in front of the Knights of Columbus Hall at Seventh and Frederica Streets. *Submitted by the Daughters of Isabella*

YOUTH RETREAT
A retreat of Catholic youth held at St. Stephen Cathedral in Owensboro, Sept. 17-20, 1940. Father Raymond J. O'Brien served as retreat master. *Submitted by Father Joe Mills and Father Phil Riney*

ST. LEO

Members of the parish and soldiers who attended the blessing and dedication of the first St. Leo Church in Murray by Bishop Francis R. Cotton in 1943. *Submitted by St. Leo Parish*

DEDICATED

The blessing and dedication of St. Leo Church in Murray happened on a windy day in the fall of 1943. This photo shows the first bishop of Owensboro, Most Rev. Francis R. Cotton, proclaiming the opening prayers of the blessing of a church upon entering the new building. *Submitted by St. Leo Parish*

JOINING PARISHES

Parishioners gather outside St. Paul Church on Fourth Street in Owensboro after a Mass in 1948. That year, St. Paul Parish and the nearby St. Joseph Parish were combined by Bishop Cotton. Masses were held at both locations the first year to ease the transition. This Mass may have been one of the last Masses at St. Joseph Parish or one of the first combined Masses of the new SS. Joseph & Paul Parish. *Submitted by Margaret Montgomery*

CHILDREN'S CHOIR

The Immaculate Conception Parish Children's Choir in Earlington sings under the direction of organist 'organist Sylvia Dunn in 1955. *Submitted by Barbara Davis for Immaculate Conception Parish*

ST. MARY

St. Mary Catholic Church in LaCenter as it looked in November 1956, when Bishop Francis R. Cotton blessed and dedicated the new building. *Submitted by Father Phil Riney*

ST. ANN

Father Joseph Spaulding presides at Mass in St. Ann Church, Morganfield, on a Sunday during the 1950s. Several details in this photo illustrate church practice for worship prior to the renewals of the Second Vatican Council which began in 1963. Notice the side altars commemorating Mary and Joseph, the parents of Jesus, the communion rail, the prominent place of statues and the priest with his back to the people, leading them in prayer. The original St. Ann Church in Morganfield was constructed in 1877 and featured a tall steeple with spires on each roof corner and around the base of the bell tower. It is a Catholic cultural custom to ring the parish church bell at 6 a.m., noon and 6 p.m. daily to call Catholics to pray the Angelus to commemorate the announcement of the Angel Gabriel to a Jewish girl named Mary that she would become the Mother of Jesus. *Submitted by St. Ann Parish*

St. Lawrence

Parishioners pray inside St. Lawrence Church in St. Lawrence during the early 1960s. In 1965, the interior of the church was remodeled under the leadership of Father Maurice Tiell, pastor at the time. *Submitted by Millie Carrico*

Outdoor Mass

St. Henry Parish in Aurora used an outdoor pavilion during the summer of 1968 for the Sunday celebration of the Mass with pastor Msgr. George Hancock presiding over an altar made of decorative bricks. *Submitted by John Sergeant for St. Henry Parish*

Lay Volunteers

Lay Extension Volunteers pose with many of the priests and sisters whom they assisted in the education of Catholic youth in Catholic schools and parishes in western Kentucky in 1965. *Submitted by Father Joe Mills*

END OF AN ERA
A parishioner watches as St. Paul Church in Leitchfield burns after being struck by lightning on Sunday, July 21, 1968. The building and contents were completely destroyed. Under the leadership of Father Richard Danhauer, a new foundation was laid in March 1969. When Father Danhauer was transferred, Father William Borntraeger surpervised the completion of the new church building and it was dedicated by Bishop Henry J. Soenneker on Dec. 21, 1969. *Submitted by Deanna Kipper*

SS. PETER & PAUL
Bishop Henry J. Soenneker, center, on the steps of SS. Peter & Paul Church in Hopkinsville at their 100th anniversary celebration in 1972. In 2002, the church and rectory were replaced with a new church building. *Submitted by Diocesan Archives*

SACRED HEART
Bishop Henry J. Soenneker speaks at Sacred Heart Parish in Hickman in Fulton County. Church history records that Bishop Soenneker offered the formal dedication for their newly constructed church on June 17, 1977, and this might be part of that celebration. The parish was originally known as St. Bridget when the first church was built in 1861. When a new church was constructed in 1890, it became known as Sacred Heart. *Submitted by Diocesan Archives*

128

DAUGHTERS IN SERVICE
Daughters of Isabella Circle #241 – the female counterpart of the Knights of Columbus – at a 1973 awards dinner in Owensboro with the second Bishop of Owensboro, Most Rev. Henry J. Soenneker, at left. This was the 50th anniversary of the group which was founded in Owensboro in 1923. *Submitted by the Daughters of Isabella*

MUSIC AT THE MOUNT
The Mount St. Joseph Summer Concert series was a popular event in Maple Mount as shown in this image from the late 1970s. Visitors are seated on the front lawn of the Mount St. Joseph motherhouse campus as the Owensboro Symphony Orchestra performs on stage. *Submitted by Debbi Hopkins*

ALTAR SOCIETY
The Altar Society of St. Joseph Parish, Bowling Green in the 1970s. Pictured left to right: Marian Grubbs, Kathryn Garrison, unknown, unknown, Bonnie Gibson, Carolyn Simon, unknown, Marian Oakes, unknown, Madge Simon, unknown, Fr. Lucian Hayden, unknown. *Submitted by Bonnie Gibson*

129

ALTAR SERVERS
Altar servers from St. Alphonsus Parish
during the 1970s.
Submitted by St. Alphonsus parish

SERRA CLUB
The Owensboro Serra Club hosts an annual
Christmas party for seminarians in 1982 at Gabe's
Restaurant in Owensboro. Seated, left to right:
Father Ed Bradley, Father Gerald Calhoun, Msgr.
Anthony Higdon, Bob Osborne, Bishop Henry
Soenneker, Father Louis Piskula (chaplain), Paul
Coomes, Joseph Hagan, Abe Walker and Herb
Bertke. Standing, left to right: Gerald Baker,
Larry Hostetter, Bob Slack, Eugene Hayden, Greg
Trawick, Miles Thomas, Henry Weider, Norbert
Greenwell, Bruce McCarty, Randolph Kramer, Tony
Jones, Bill Booth, Marty Hayes, Charlie Russelburg,
Joe Castlen, Harold Clark, Dennis Jacobs, Gary
Payne, Danny Goff, Bruce Fogle, Jack Wilson,
Dick Weafer, Larry McBride, Bruce Galloway, Dick
Greenwell, Kevin Osborne, Jim Eaton, Richard
Booth, Richard Cash, Paul McConnell, and Father
Pat Bittel. *Submitted by Owensboro Serra Club*

RESTORED
A Mass was celebrated on Palm Sunday 1986 in Saint
Pius Tenth Church, Owensboro, after a renovation of
the parish church. The altar position was moved to the
west side of the building from the rear of the church,
shown here with doorways. In this way the altar faces
the east, as does the priest, as he leads the faithful in
prayer. *Submitted by Saint Pius Tenth Parish*

BLUE ARMY
Bishop Henry J. Soenneker speaks to a gathering of The Blue Army of Our Lady of Fatima. The Blue Army, the World Apostolate of Mary, is a worldwide public association of the faithful, responding to the requests that Our Blessed Mother made to three shepherd children in 1917 in Fatima, Portugal, to help save souls and bring peace to the world. It promotes Eucharistic prayer and the Rosary, as well as penance and generous acceptance of the duties of our state in life.
Submitted by Diocesan Archives

DEDICATION
The dedication Mass for the new Sacred Heart Church in Hickman on June 17, 1977. The dedication was led by Bishop Henry J. Soenneker.
Submitted by Diocesan Archives

ROSARY CHAPEL
Bishop John J. McRaith, seated at center, visited Rosary Chapel in Paducah on Aug. 18, 1984. Rosary Chapel Parish was established in 1947 by Father Albert Thompson, pastor of St. Francis de Sales Church. Because segregation prevailed at that time, Father Thompson felt that Paducah's Black Catholics had no sense of identity at St. Francis, and needed a parish of their own. The first Mass at Rosary Chapel was offered in the spring of 1947 and the school opened in September that same year. Father Richard Wersing, C.S.S.P. was the first pastor. Ursuline sisters from Maple Mount taught and maintained the school. A close-knit family spirit, openness, a spirit of fellowship and justifiable pride characterized Rosary Chapel from the beginning. The doors have always been open to all races. This continually attracts growing numbers of people to religious services and parish activities. Besides being one of the most beautiful churches in the area, Rosary Chapel's liturgical services with gospel music attract many visitors. *Submitted by Diocesan Archives*

131

St. Joseph
Bishop John J. McRaith, front left, visited St. Joseph Catholic Center in Greenville on Oct. 12, 1986. The center is part of St. Joseph parish in Central City. *Submitted by Diocesan Archives*

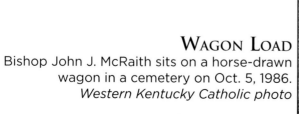

Celebration at St. Agnes
Bishop Soenneker cuts the ribbon on St. Agnes Church in Uniontown. The ribbon cutting was in either 1975 or 1981 – when major renovation projects were completed. *Submitted by Diocesan Archives*

Wagon Load
Bishop John J. McRaith sits on a horse-drawn wagon in a cemetery on Oct. 5, 1986. *Western Kentucky Catholic photo*

HOLY WATER

Bishop John J. McRaith sprinkles holy water at a Mass at St. Pius X Church in Calvert City on June 1, 1986.
Western Kentucky Catholic photo

CENTENNIAL

Sister Paulette McCarty, O.S.U., speaks at the 100th anniversary of St. Joseph parish in Central City in 1986. Father Carl Wise, C.P.P.S., Bishop John J. McRaith and Father Harold Diller are seated beside her. The parish was known as St. Martin when the first church was built in 1886. When a new church building was dedicated in 1912, the name was changed to St. Joseph. *Submitted by Diocesan Archives*

MAKING WAY FOR PROGRESS

St. Mary of the Woods parishioners watch as the Monsignor Hugh O'Sullivan Building at their church in Whitesville is razed in 1987.
Western Kentucky Catholic photo by Mel Howard

TRAINING THE TRAINERS
Sister Sharon Grant, S.C.N., leads a RENEW "Training of the Trainers" workshop in a meeting room at Saint Anthony Church in Peonia in 1984. Bishop John McRaith brought the RENEW process to the diocese in 1984 to help parishes better organize themselves as a community of small communities. Sister Sharon Grant was the Director of RENEW. *Submitted by Diocesan Archives*

THE CHEFS
Floyd Russelburg, left, and Dave Clark cook pork for the St. Mary of the Woods Parish picnic in July 1986. *Western Kentucky Catholic photo by Mel Howard*

AFTER THE FIRE
Father Tony Ziegler comforts parishioners after a fire destroyed the church building at St. Columba in Lewisport on Aug. 9, 1989. Parishioners, left to right: Eva Howard, Zita Johnson and Mary Emmick. *Western Kentucky Catholic photo by Mel Howard*

SESQUICENTENNIAL MASS

A sesquicentennial Mass, lead by Bishop John J. McRaith, was held at St. John the Evangelist in Paducah on April 30, 1989. Front row, left to right: Father Harold Diller, Father Vic Boarman, Father Robert Drury, Father Anthony Higdon and Father John Vaughan. Second row, left to right: Father Richard Danhauer, Father Joe Trapp, Father Joe Bomensatt, Bishop McRaith, Father Frank Roof, Father Richard Clements and Father Lucian Hayden. Back row, left to right: Father Henry Willett, Father Ben Luther and Father Bruce Fogle.
Submitted by Diocesan Archives

HIGH ALTAR

Bishop John J. McRaith in front of the altar at SS. Peter & Paul Church in Hopkinsville during a visit there on June 18, 1991. The beautiful high altar was used in the church sanctuary from 1898 until 2002. When the new church was built in 2002, the altar and other cherished artifacts were placed in the bell tower room. James Westin carved the altar in 1898.
Submitted by Diocesan Archives

BIG MOVE

Bishop John J. McRaith loads a podium into the back of a pickup truck during the Catholic Pastoral Center's move to 600 Locust Street in Owensboro in June 1990.
Western Kentucky Catholic photo

St. John

Parishioners gather before Mass at
St. John Church in Sunfish in 1990.
Photo by Mel Howard

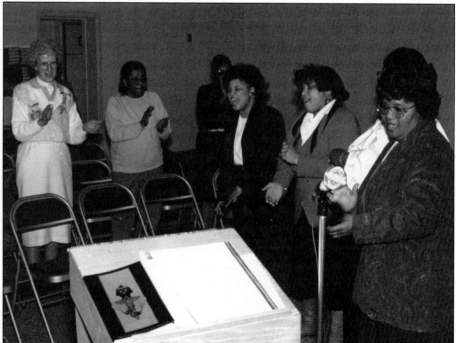

Blessed Sacrament Chapel

The Martin Luther King, Jr., Day celebration at Blessed
Sacrament Chapel in Owensboro in February 1994. Sister
Margaret Turk is at left and Gloria Adams is at right.
Submitted by Diocesan Archives

WORLD YOUTH DAY
During World Youth Day in August 1993, in Denver, Colo., Father Richard Powers, standing at right, accompanied a few hundred diocesan youth to pray with Pope John Paul II. At center are Owensboro seminarians Brian Johnson, David Kennedy and Ken Mikulcik – who were all later ordained as priests for the Diocese of Owensboro – as they awoke on a crisp, cool, morning with thousands of young people around them. *Submitted by Debbi Hopkins*

NEW PASTOR
Pastors of Catholic parishes are installed for ministry among the people of a Catholic community by the diocesan bishop. Here, Bishop John McRaith installed Father Richard Meredith as pastor of Saint Pius Tenth Parish in Owensboro at a weekend liturgy on January 3, 2001. *Submitted by Saint Pius Tenth Church*

ST. BENEDICT CHURCH

A Mass at St. Benedict in Wax in May 1994. Grayson County
is served by three Catholic churches, St. Benedict in Wax,
St. Anthony in Peonia and St. Augustine in Grayson Springs.
Western Kentucky Catholic photo by Mel Howard

LOURDES

Father John Meredith speaks to parishioners outside Our Lady of Lourdes Church in
Owensboro on Sept. 15, 1996. Parishioners drawn from Blessed Mother and Immaculate
Parishes in Owensboro attended the first Mass celebrated at Our Lady of Lourdes Church
on Sept. 6, 1959. Father Meredith was installed as the fourth pastor for the parish in 1995.
Submitted by Diocesan Archives

BURGOO BREAK
Owensboro's Blessed Mother burgoo team takes a break at the International Bar-B-Q Festival on the Owensboro riverfront in May 1995.
Submitted by Diocesan Archives

FATHER EMMANUELLE
Father Jim Emmanuelle speaks to a packed Mass at St. Mary of the Woods Church in Whitesville on Sept. 29, 1996.
Western Kentucky Catholic photo by Mel Howard

BLESSING FOR TRINITY HIGH SCHOOL
Father Marty Hayes, Father B.J. Hagman and Father Richard Powers blessing a hallway of Trinity High School in Whitesville on April 7, 1997.
Submitted by Diocesan Archives

DOG DAYS

A boy carries his dog at a picnic at St. Ann Church in Morganfield on Oct. 3, 1997. *Submitted by Diocesan Archives*

CELEBRATION

The congregation joins hands while praying the "Our Father" during a Mass to celebrate the 175th anniversary of St. Lawrence Church in St. Lawrence on Aug. 10, 1997. *Submitted by Diocesan Archives*

FANCY FARM

Bishop John J. McRaith speaks to Senator Wendell H. Ford minutes before delivering the invocation at the Fancy Farm picnic in 1998. Fancy Farm is home to St. Denis Church and St. Jerome Church. *Western Kentucky Catholic photo*

New Beginnning

After a year of construction and eager anticipation, the new church and parish hall of St. Mary Parish in Franklin is dedicated on Aug. 8, 1999. Bishop John J. McRaith prays at the entrance to the church near the Baptismal font during the dedication. The Baptismal font was replaced by a Baptismal pool in 2009. Standing, left to right: Father Dennis Holly, pastor of St. Mary, servers Keith Kinder, Mallory McBride and Anthony Stoll (holding book), Bishop McRaith and Father Darrell Venters. *Submitted by St. Mary Parish Archive*

Benediction

Father Ray Clark offers the benediction at St. Joseph in Mayfield on Oct. 3, 1997. *Submitted by Diocesan Archives*

Breaking New Ground

St. Mary parishioners gather for a ground-breaking ceremony on Sept. 20, 1998, for their new, larger church and fellowship hall. The 9,700-square-foot structure was attached to the north side of the stone church and basement which was built in 1953, at 403 North Main Street in Franklin. Foreground: Server Anthony Stoll and Father Frank Ruff, interim pastor. Other adults, left to right: Charlene Moore, Gene Roberts, Anna Marie Roberts, two unidentified guests, David Fowler, Jim Collins, Richard Johnson, Dean Henderson, Steve Maloney and Jean Whilhite. Servers David Brown and Ashley Stoll are standing at right. Henderson and Maloney served as co-chairmen of the building committee which included Anna Marie Roberts, Fowler, Johnson, Collins, Wilhite and Frank Farmer (not visible in the photo). *Submitted by St. Mary Parish Archive*

BRINGING THE LIGHT
Kevin Steele, left, gets a little help from Jake Mauzy in lighting a difficult candle at Holy Name of Jesus Church in Henderson on Aug. 30, 1998. *Western Kentucky Catholic photo by Mel Howard*

PAPAL VISIT
Paul O'Bryan meets Pope John Paul II in Denver, Colo., during World Youth Day in 1993. Paul O'Bryan's wife, Frances Boswell O'Bryan, stands at right. His daughter, Judy Basham, is also pictured. *Western Kentucky Catholic photo*

DEDICATION
Sister Rose Marita O'Bryan, O.S.U., places a crucifix on a wall after it had been blessed by Bishop John McRaith during a dedication ceremony of the renovated Mount St. Joseph Retreat Center on April 26, 1998. Several crucifixes were blessed in the ceremony and placed in various rooms of the renovated main building, which also received some additions during the construction. *Messenger-Inquirer photo by Bryan Leazenby*

LONELY LANDMARK

St. Stephen Church at Land Between the Lakes was the only church not torn down when Kentucky and Barkley Lakes were built. Parishioners did have to vacate the church for the lake project, though, and built a new church with the same name in Cadiz. This photo was taken on Jan. 27, 1998.
Photo by Mel Howard

DINNER WITH CAYWOOD

Holy Name Men's Club members Ray Thompson, left, Commie Clancy and Rodney Woodward prepare meals for a "Dinner with Caywood" benefit for the parish's endowment fund on Aug. 30, 1998. Caywood Ledford was the keynote speaker for the event and was accompanied by University of Kentucky basketball players, including Walter McCarty and Tony Delk.
Western Kentucky Catholic photo by Mel Howard

143

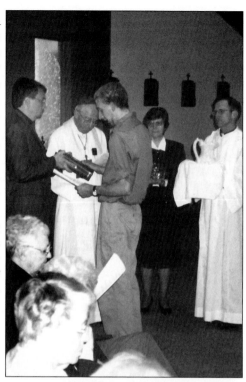

Lay Minister
Aaron Jahn was commissioned as a professional Lay Minister by Bishop John J. McRaith in May 2000 at Brescia University. Looking on are Brescia faculty members, from left, Father Larry Hostetter, Sister Cheryl Clemons, O.S.U., and Father Pat Ryan, director of the Brescia lay ministry program. *Submitted by Debbi Hopkins*

Chop Shop
Sister Georgetta Higdon, 91, right, laughs with Sister Marian Powers on Tuesday as they chop enough onions for 35 gallons of homemade coleslaw. The Mount St. Joseph Ursuline sisters are preparing for the annual benefit picnic to be held in September 1998 at Maple Mount. The picnic raises money to help support retired sisters at Maple Mount. *Messenger-Inquirer photo by Cathy Clarke*

Pit Master
Bishop John J. McRaith coats chickens with dip at a Parish barbecue in the Diocese. *Western Kentucky Catholic photo*

NATIVITY

Allie Edge and Frank Montgomery portray St. Mary and St. Joseph as Laura Payne, as the Angel Gabriel, standing, looks on. They created the nativity scene in 2005 at St. John the Baptist Church in Fordsville. *Submitted by Margaret Montgomery*

CONVOCATION

Members of Saint Pius Tenth Parish, Owensboro, posing with pastor Father Richard Meredith, front right, in the Catholic Pastoral Center during a Convocation held in August 2000. *Submitted by Saint Pius Tenth Parish*

PASSIONIST OBLATES

Father Joe Mills and Father Louis Piskula posed with the first group of Passionist Oblates commissioned in 2001 – after a four-year formation period – by the Passionist Nuns of St. Joseph Monastery near Whitesville. While remaining involved in the ordinary affairs of the world, Passionist Oblates pursue a life of holiness in the spirit of the Passionist community in ways compatible with their state in life. *Submitted by Father Joe Mills*

145

WELCOME HOME

Habitat for Humanity volunteer executive director Virginia Braswell, center, smiles with volunteers from the Diocese of Owensboro as they celebrate the 15th anniversary of the organization at an Owensboro Deanery build on Cedar Street in Owensboro in 2003. *Submitted by Ruth Ann Carrico*

HAPPY HOME

Father John Vaughn presents a Bible to the recipient of a Habitat for Humanity home built on Cedar Street in Owensboro by donations and volunteers from the Owensboro Catholic Deanery in 2003. *Submitted by Ruth Ann Carrico*

LADIES GUILD

The Ladies Guild of St. Mary Catholic Church in Franklin hosts a Tasters' Luncheon each year in April and October. This event is generously supported by the community and other churches. More than 200 guests select from a bountiful buffet of meats, vegetables, salads, breads, desserts and drinks prepared by the ladies and men of the Parish. The luncheons are the Guild's main fund raiser and the profit is used to assist the needy in the parish and community, to provide refreshments and gifts for sacramental receptions and to help pay for improvements to the new church, such as new pews and carpet. These ladies are tired but happy that another successful Tasters' Luncheon has been completed. Left to right: Lois Oshefsky, Rosemary Estep, Adrianna Lebbin, Becky Clark, Guild President Tracee Cremeens, Joann Bradford, Colleen Rafferty and Mae King. *Submitted by St. Mary Parish Archive*

An Ending

St. John the Baptist parish was formed in Ohio County in 1893, but moved to Fordsville in the 1960s in a mobile chapel. The permanent church building was dedicated in 1976. It was a sad, yet joyful, moment 30 years later as parishioners concluded the final Mass in their church in 2006. Their next service was held in the new church just across the street and the old church was converted into a parish hall. *Submitted by Margaret Montgomery*

New Light

The congregation gathers in semi-darkness at the dedication of the new St. John the Baptist Church in Fordsville in 2006. The new church was lit with new light for the first time once the procession of light brought candles to light the altar and sanctuary and a lit candle was presented to Bishop John J. McRaith. Many friends and visitors from Baptist, Methodist and Church of God denominations joined the congregation for the dedication Mass. *Submitted by Diocesan Archives*

New Beginning
Parishioners file into the new St. John the Baptist Church on Smith Street in Fordsville in August 2006. The old church was located across the street and was converted into the first parish hall. *Submitted by Margaret Montgomery*

PRAYER VIGIL

Sister Isabel González of Paducah leans over the pew to take a picture of the Most Rev. John McRaith and the Most Rev. Gerald Gettelfinger, the bishops of Owensboro and Evansville, on Aug. 28, 2006, during an interfaith prayer vigil for comprehensive immigration reform at St. Stephen Cathedral.
Messenger-Inquirer photo by John Dunham

HONEY AND LOCUSTS

St. John the Baptist Parish in Fordsville built a new church which opened in 2006. Blue stained glass doors and windows throughout the building depict important items or events from the life of St. John. This window features a honey pot.
Submitted by Margaret Montgomery

CARMELITE CHARITY

Sister Dorothy Marie Willett, right, speaks with Helen Murphy during Murphy's 89th Birthday party at the Carmel Home in Owensboro in August 2004. Helen Murphy moved into the Carmel Home in 2002. The Carmel Home is a nursing facility established and operated by Carmelite Sisters of the Divine Heart of Jesus as a "home away from home" for the elderly, regardless of church affiliation.
Submitted by Peggy McCarthy

PICNIC AT THE MOUNT

Rick Blandford with the St. Alphonsus Catholic Church cooking team sprays the barbecue pits on Sept. 13, 2009, as the last of the 3,000 pounds of mutton and pork are carried to the hungry people at the annual Mount St. Joseph Picnic to benefit the Ursuline Sisters of Mount Saint Joseph. The 700 barbecued chickens were all gone within an hour of the start of serving.
Messenger-Inquirer photo by Gary Emord-Netzley

BLOCK PARTY

SS. Joseph & Paul Parish in Owensboro hosts their annual Block Party outside the parish hall on East Fourth Street for the neighbors of the parish. The event provides food, clothing, haircuts and other services for the needy. This photo shows the church, the parish hall and hundreds of people who celebrated with the parish in 2009. *Submitted by April Dickens*

OUR LADY OF MOUNT CARMEL

Sister M. Andrea, a resident of the Carmel Home, takes photos of the newly-installed statue of Mary in front of the home's chapel at 2501 Old Hartford Road on April 26, 2010. The 4,500-square foot chapel was constructed in 2009. Ghislain Aubin, a project manager for King Richard's New and Antique Religious Artifacts of Alpharetta, Ga., said his company had the six-foot marble statue of Mary made for the Carmel Home. The Carmel Home is a Roman Catholic personal care and nursing home operated by Carmelite Sisters of the Divine Heart of Jesus.
Messenger-Inquirer photo by Jenny Sevcik

Altar at Christmas
The altar at St. William Church in Knottsville at Christmas in 2009. *Submitted by Millie Carrico*

Sesquicentennial Celebration
The 150th anniversary of St. Joseph Church, Bowling Green, was celebrated on March 22, 2009. Shown left to right are: Father Ray Clark, Father Maurice Tiell, Deacon Bob Imel, Father Jerry Riney, Diocesan Administrator Very Reverend J. Michael Clark, Father Pat Reynolds, Father Stan Puryear, Father Anthoni Ottagon, H.G.N., Father Joe Mills and Father Richard Powers. *Submitted by Bonnie Gibson*

Show of Respect
The Tabernacle stands in the center of the altar at St. Lawrence Church in St. Lawrence in 2009. Upon entering the church, Catholics genuflect toward the Tabernacle on their right knee or by bowing the head if unable to kneel. This is done out of respect for the Blessed Sacrament residing inside. *Submitted by Millie Carrico*

Prayer Warriors

St. Michael the Archangel Cenacle, of St. Mary Parish in Franklin, made a pilgrimage to The Dominican Sisters of St. Cecilia Congregation in Nashville, Tenn., on Feb. 28, 2009. Sister Mary Angelia was the tour guide through the congregation's beautiful new chapel, the old chapel, the parlors and heritage room. Mark Pais, a St. Mary parishioner, was the construction superintendent for their new chapel for Hardaway Construction of Nashville, Tenn. After the tour the pilgrims returned to the new chapel to pray the Chaplet of Divine Mercy and the Prayer to St. Michael. St. Michael the Archangel Cenacle members meet monthly in church before the exposed Blessed Sacrament or in a member's home to begin a Novena selected by the group, to pray the Chaplet of Divine Mercy, the Rosary and Prayer to St. Michael for the Parish "that our little Parish of St. Mary will be all that God desires us to be" and for other intentions. In addition to the pilgrimage to the Chapel of St. Cecilia, the group has also made a pilgrimage to the Diocesan Shrine in Bowling Green. Cenacle members are "Prayer Warriors" who devote many hours to prayer and to adoration of the Blessed Sacrament – an essential aspect of parish life. Pilgrims, left to right: Dean Henderson, Patty Kinder, Sharon and Steve Maloney, Tracee Cremeens, Carol Darrow, Emma Cremeens, Father Robert Drury, Abbey Pais, Mark Pais and Miranda Cremeens. Their guide Sister Mary Angelia is in front. Photo by Sharon Henderson. *Submitted by St. Mary Parish Archive*

KNIGHTS

Members of the Knights of Columbus Council #12009 from Our Lady of Lourdes Parish, Owensboro, posed with pastor Father Brad Whistle after a meeting in the spring of 2010.
Submitted by Our Lady of Lourdes Parish

KNIGHTS

This statue of St. Lawrence stands in the sanctuary at St. Lawrence Church.
Submitted by Millie Carrico

PIETA GROTTO

The Pieta grotto in a small grove of trees behind Christ The King Church in Madisonville. Catholics maintain such shrines and statues to remind them to pray and petition for help in their lives through the intercession of the saints.
Submitted by Christ The King Parish

HEALING COMFORT OF JESUS
Inmates at the Kentucky State Penitentiary sing "Happy Birthday" to Paul Stevens. As a Prison Minister for Resurrection Catholic Parish in Dawson Springs, Stevens made weekly visits to inmates during the 1990s and early 2000s. He frequently led the men in prayer in the prison chapel and, for many of them, he brought the presence of Jesus' healing comfort into their spiritual lives. Among those he ministered to was death row inmate Harold McQueen before his execution in 1997. *Evansville Courier & Press photo by Denny Simmons, submitted by Pat Solomon*

DEDICATED SERVICE
Paul Stevens of Dawson Springs Resurrection Parish climbs the steep, stone steps in front of the "Castle on Lake Barkley," Kentucky State Penitentiary. Stevens visited the facility's inmates weekly for many years. *Evansville Courier & Press photo by Denny Simmons, submitted by Pat Solomon*

ST. HENRY
A 2010 Sunday celebration of Mass at St. Henry Church in Aurora with pastor Father Babu Kulathumkal Joseph, H.G.N., presiding. The church was built in 1983. *Submitted by John Sergeant for St. Henry Parish*

Coming Together

Almost every parish in the Diocese of Owensboro helps the Ursuline Sisters with the Mount Saint Joseph barbecue picnic each year in Maple Mount. In this 2009 photo, servers work the stands to keep the hungry crowd fed. In 1874, five Ursuline Sisters came from Louisville to establish a school in western Daviess County. The Ursuline Sisters of Mount Saint Joseph are religious women who live an apostolic life supported by prayer and contemplation. They proclaim Jesus to all people through the ministry of education and Christian formation. They minister in the states of Kentucky, Illinois, Kansas, Louisiana, Minnesota, Missouri, New Mexico and Tennessee, in the District of Columbia and in Chile, South America. *Submitted by Diocese Archive*

Living Faith in a Diverse Culture

Parishioners of Holy Trinity Catholic Church in Morgantown met March 21, 2010, to plan their participation in a Hispanic Congress called "Unity in Diversity: Faith and Culture in This Reality," to be held in Paducah. *Submitted by Diocesan Archives*

Belonging to God

Bishop William Francis Medley makes the sign of the cross in ashes on the forehead of 3-year-old Paul Clayton as his mother, Michelle Clayton stands behind him during Mass on Ash Wednesday, Feb. 17, 2010, at St. Stephen Cathedral in Owensboro. "This smudge means I belong to God," Bishop Medley told the parishioners during his homily. *Messenger-Inquirer photo by Gary Emord-Netzley*